ROYAL MUSICAL ASSOCIATION
MONOGRAPHS
12

Salomon and the Burneys

Private Patronage and a Public Career

IAN WOODFIELD

ROYAL MUSICAL ASSOCIATION

ASHGATE

Published for the Royal Musical Association by
Ashgate Publishing Limited
Gower House
Croft Road
Aldershot
Hants GU11 3HR
England

Ashgate Publishing Company
Suite 420
101 Cherry Street
Burlington, VT 05401-4405
USA   100522283X

Ashgate website: http://www.ashgate.com

British Library Cataloguing in Publication Data
Woodfield, Ian
   Salomon and the Burneys : private patronage and a public
   career. – (Royal Musical Association monographs)
   1. Salomon, Johann Peter – Career in music 2. Burney (Family)
   3. Music patronage – England – London – History – 18th
   century 4. Violinists – Germany – Biography 5. Impresarios –
   Germany – Biography
   I. Title
   780.9'2

Library of Congress Cataloging-in-Publication Data
Woodfield, Ian.
   Salomon and the Burneys : private patronage and a public career / Ian
   Woodfield.
      p. cm. – (Royal Musical Association monographs ; no. 12)
   Includes bibliographical references and index.
   ISBN 0-7546-3612-7 (alk. paper)
      1. Salomon, John Peter, 1745–1815. 2. Burney family. 3.
   Impresarios–England–London–Biography. 4. Violinists–Biography. 5.
   Music–England–London–18th century–History and criticism. I. Title. II. Series.

ML429.S14 W66 2003
780'.92–dc21
[B]
                                                                        2002043694

ISBN 0 7546 3612 7

Typeset by IML Typographers, Birkenhead, Merseyside, and printed in
Great Britain by MPG Books Ltd, Bodmin, Cornwall.

Contents

Introduction

The world in which professional musicians had to make their living in late eighteenth-century England was a sharply divided one: on the one hand, there was the public stage, represented by the magnificent Pantheon and its high-society concerts, the King's Theatre with its aristocratic patronage and its intoxicating, circus-like emphasis on star performers, the elegant concert room at Hanover Square and the impressive Handel Commemorations at Westminster Abbey; on the other, equally important, was the private domain of the domestic lesson, the morning quartet party, the fashionable evening soirée and the summer country weekend, when professional musicians could walk, fish or make music with wealthy amateur enthusiasts. Distinct though these two aspects of musical life may now seem, they were far from unrelated. Indeed, there has probably never been a period in which the public and private spheres of professional musical activity were so closely interrelated. In a later age, it would be possible for a talented musician to develop a successful career on the concert platform through direct contact with the public by means of newspaper advertisements, planted puffs, reviews and handbills. In the eighteenth century such an approach was risky. Neither for a subscription series nor for an individual benefit could publicity of this kind be relied upon to bring in an audience of sufficient size to ensure a return on money and time invested. A substantial element of the concert-going public still consisted of private patrons, whose support was best obtained through personal contact.[1] The implication for musicians, especially for those at the top of their profession, was clear: social savoir-faire – the ability to conduct oneself with propriety in aristocratic circles – was every bit as important as technical proficiency or musicianship in building a career.

The relationship between the social and professional sides of the music profession is most evident when a striking failure in one adversely affected the other. An interesting case of a talented musician failing socially is Antonio Lolli, one of the most technically

I am most grateful to Simon McVeigh for supplying me with a list of references to Salomon in London concert advertisements before 1791 from his database *Calendar of London Concerts 1750–1800*, Goldsmiths' College, University of London. This source, together with his published work on the Professional Concert, has been an indispensable aid.

[1]   During his year in London, Leopold Mozart spent much more time promoting his children at private soirées than he did in arranging public concerts for them. See Ian Woodfield, 'New Light on the Mozarts' London Visit: A Private Concert with Manzuoli', *Music and Letters*, 75 (1995), 187–208.

accomplished violinists of the age, who arrived in London early in 1785 with every reason to expect success. A reviewer commented that his playing was brilliant if somewhat eccentric: 'LOLLI, as far outshone by Cramer and Giardini in the superior excellencies of the violin, *taste* and *pathos*, as he outdoes them in excentric oddity, trick and voluble execution, is esteemed at the highest rate in some foreign countries.'[2] Despite ranking him 'a very great, expressive, and admirable performer', Burney stated that some social difficulty ('a caprice in his conduct') led to his being 'seldom heard'.[3] His early departure from England ('sudden and à la sourdine') was apparently to enable him to escape a substantial debt owed to his fellow violinist Salpietro.[4] But in a very frank letter to her sister Susan, Charlotte Burney reveals that the version of events recorded in *A General History of Music* was far from the whole truth, and that the violinist had in fact seriously offended Burney himself:

St. Martin's Street 15 January 1784[5]   Charlotte Burney to Susan Burney

Lolli, the very celebrated violin player from Germany, brought my Father some letters from Mr Ebeling,[5] & Miss Mathias, & my Father call'd upon him, & I sent a Note (before he made his party) to invite him here, & his answer was 'that he would not fail' upon wch all this party was invited professedly to meet him – but at three o'clock *the very day*, came an ill written French note from Sig^r Lolli, to say he was sorry he had forgot an *ancient* engagement, & c^d not come, but that he w^d be glad to come another time! This was tolerably provoking to be sure – & absolute impertinence, for supposing that it was true that he *had* forgot another Engagement he might have come in for an hour to shew his good will! But young La Trobe says he was notorious in Germany for his Caprice – My Father, as you may imagine, was greatly incensed – two days after the gentleman called here, & left a card – two days after that, sent in the morning to know 'what was the most likely part of the day to find Dr Burney at home?' My Father was at home *then*, & only sent word 'that he was going out for the whole day' which dry answer has put an end to all intercourse with the great Lolli for the present.[6]

Burney's residence was a notable gathering-place for musicians of all kinds. Relations between hosts and guests were high-spirited and friendly, with much good-humoured musical banter. Having

[2] *Public Advertiser*, 18 February 1785. Cited in Simon McVeigh, *Concert Life in London from Mozart to Haydn* (Cambridge, 1993), 146. There was something of a vogue for party tricks on the violin. In a letter to her sister Susan dated 15 January 1784[5], Charlotte Burney wrote that 'a gentlemanlike young man' named Mr Head had played 'all sorts of tricks on the fiddle'. He expressed 'Howdyo do? & *very well thank you*, very intelligibly on the fiddle'. London, British Library, Egerton MS 3700A, f. 129.

[3] Charles Burney, *A General History of Music from the Earliest Ages to the Present Period*, ed. Frank Mercer, 2 vols. (London, 1935; repr. 1957), ii, 1020.

[4] *Public Advertiser*, 20 May 1785. Cited by Simon McVeigh, *The Violinist in London's Concert Life* (New York, 1989), 118.

[5] Christoph Daniel Ebeling, translator of Burney's *Tours* and an important German correspondent. See *The Letters of Charles Burney*, ed. Alvaro Ribeiro, i: 1751–1784 (Oxford, 1991), 115.

[6] British Library, Egerton MS 3700A, f. 129.

committed a serious breach of social etiquette, however, Lolli found himself pointedly excluded, and he discovered to his cost that his thoughtless action would not be lightly forgiven. Burney exercised considerable influence in the London musical world, and the violinist's prospects might well have been damaged by the affair, especially since a reputation for 'caprice' or 'impertinence', once acquired, was difficult to shake off. The age of the temperamental virtuoso, waited on by admiring aristocratic patrons, was some time in the future, except perhaps for the top superstars of Italian opera. After a few more public engagements Lolli left England.

A sadder case altogether, illustrating the negative impact that professional decline could have on social relationships, was the composer Sacchini, whose diminishing status during his last London years badly affected his once warm relations with the Burney family. For so long the idol of the Italian opera establishment at the King's Theatre, he had fallen on hard times. Fanny Burney met him in July 1781 and was shocked at the change:

Sacchini is the mere ghost of what he was, in almost every respect; so altered a man in so few years I never saw. I should not even have known him had his name not been spoken; and the same ill-health which has so much impaired his person, and robbed him of more beauty than any other man ever possessed, seems also to have impaired his mental faculties.[7]

She now no longer found him 'pleasant' even when he tried to be 'gay', and she was struck by the way in which the 'good breeding we so much admired in him' had degenerated into 'too much obsequiousness'. This regrettable change of character, she thought, could be attributed to the decline in his professional circumstances, notably 'his continual distress for money'. The bluntness of this link between 'good breeding' and financial success on the one hand and 'obsequiousness' and debt on the other strikes a rather chilling note. Sacchini was having to slip out of the country quietly to avoid his creditors. Fanny Burney mused on his fate:

That a man of such extraordinary merit, after so many years giving to this country such works as must immortalise him, should at last be forced to steal away from it, made me, I must own, feel more compassion for him than a man whose own misconduct has been the sole occasion of his distresses has any fair claim to. But to see talents which to all the world can give such delight, so useless to the owner, is truly melancholy.

She then confessed that she had deliberately altered her attitude to him: 'He seemed both gratified and surprised by my civility and attention to him, which he must long have observed were withdrawn, and which nothing but my present pity for him would have revived.' With a measure of warmth momentarily restored, the two recalled their days

7 *Diary and Letters of Madame D'Arblay (1778–1840)*, ed. Charlotte Barrett, introduction and notes by Austin Dobson, 6 vols. (London, 1904), ii, 20–1.

with Millico, and Sacchini sang through arias from four of his London operas, the exertion causing him some 'pain and fatigue'.[8]

Tragic cases of once highly regarded musicians having to rely upon charitable support in their later years are all too common in the eighteenth century; stories of lasting success are altogether rarer. A performer whose professional and social reputation had not significantly diminished at the time of his death was Johann Peter Salomon, the celebrated violinist and impresario. By all accounts a polished 'performer' in society, Salomon quickly made his mark with upper-class English socialites. As McVeigh has pointed out, he enjoyed the important advantage of being one of the large group of foreign musicians in England who, 'brought up in the obsequious atmosphere of continental courts, were masters of the correct tone to adopt, cultivated yet respectful'.[9] Rohr's comments on why English aristocrats preferred foreign musicians might have been written with him specifically in mind: 'they gave the appearance of having a social, cultural and educational status which distinguished them from their English colleagues'; they had 'foreign accents, the appearance of cosmopolitanism, sometimes a familiarity with several languages, and ingratiating manners'.[10] According to the author of the short obituary published in the *Harmonicon* in 1830, Salomon deployed all these social advantages to immediate effect. Having arrived in England in 1781, his 'letters of introduction' quickly made him known to 'all the amateurs of the day', whereupon his 'cheerful disposition' and 'great good sense' soon won for him 'the friendship of those who at first patronised him on account of his professional talents'.[11] This idealized account recognizes the relationship between Salomon's social and professional success, but its benign view of the competitive world of the late eighteenth-century London music profession is unconvincing. The harsh reality was rather different. Like so many talented players, Salomon made a promising start to his career in England, and for a few years he could reasonably have been described as one of London's leading violinists, in status broadly equivalent to Giardini or Cramer. But to sustain a position in the competitive field of top leaderships was very difficult, and there is

---

[8]   The circumstances of Sacchini's departure from England have caused some confusion. In *The New Grove Dictionary of Music and Musicians*, ed. Stanley Sadie and John Tyrrell, 29 vols. (2nd, rev. edn, London, 2001), xvi, 370, David di Chiera states: 'Faced with the threat of imprisonment, Sacchini left England in 1781 and went to Paris.' The source of this is clearly the passage from Fanny Burney cited above, in which she states that Sacchini was having 'to steal away privately, lest his creditors should stop him'. Assuming that Fanny Burney's date of 1781 for this meeting was not an error, Sacchini returned to England for one final season, no longer, apparently, under threat of imprisonment. His final departure from England in June 1782 came in the wake of the plagiarism controversy with Rauzzini.

[9]   McVeigh, *Concert Life*, 209.

[10] Deborah A. Rohr, 'A Profession of Artisans: The Careers and Social Status of British Musicians 1750–1850', (Ph.D. dissertation, University of Pennsylvania, 1983), 98.

[11] Anon., 'Memoir of Johann Peter Salomon', *Harmonicon*, 8 (1830), 45–7. See McVeigh, *Concert Life*, 187–8.

much evidence to suggest that by the late 1780s his career as a public leader was in decline. The triumph with Haydn in 1791 (which irrevocably transformed his reputation and his prospects), far from being the culminating achievement of a career in the ascendant, represents rather an unusual and striking resurrection of one on the wane. Those who, like the author of the 'Memoir', later sought to portray his early years in London as the unproblematic preamble to the recruitment of Haydn, were promoting a legend: Salomon as the heroic figure who single-handedly brought the great composer to London.

The aim of the present study is to provide a reassessment of Salomon's uneven career in London during the 1780s. This was a fiercely competitive period in the world of London concert and opera politics, and Salomon struggled to win a position as regular leader of a prestigious subscription series to rival Cramer and the Professional Concert. The public aspect of this campaign, which culminated in the Haydn visits, has been intensively researched. The sources are well known and only a brief indication of the most important of them need be given here. H. C. Robbins Landon's panoramic survey of Haydn's life provides the central documentary resource for the London visits.[12] In addition there are articles by Roscoe on the earlier attempts to attract Haydn to London and by Oldman on the composer's celebrated quarrel with Cramer and the Professional Concert.[13] A major study by McVeigh has clarified the institutional context of Haydn's visits by providing comprehensive documentation of the Professional Concert, which under Cramer's leadership was the main rival to Salomon both before and after the arrival of Haydn.[14] The recent study of Italian opera in London has shed much light on the operatic background to the composer's first London visit.[15] My own work has drawn attention to the significance of the alliance between the music-seller John Bland and Salomon in the period before the successful recruitment of Haydn.[16]

Sources which illustrate the private side of Salomon's career in the 1780s are on the whole less well known. Twining's informative and lively letters to Burney, some entries in John Marsh's lengthy diary and several letters in the correspondence of the Anglo-Indian Fowke family

---

[12]   H. C. Robbins Landon, *Haydn at Esterháza 1766–1790* (London, 1978); *Haydn in England 1791–1795* (London, 1976).

[13]   Christopher Roscoe, 'Haydn and London in the 1780s', *Music and Letters*, 49 (1968), 203–12; Cecil B. Oldman, 'Haydn's Quarrel with the "Professionals" in 1788', *Musik und Verlag: Karl Vötterle zum 65. Geburtstag am 12. April 1968*, ed. Richard Baum and Wolfgang Rehm (Kassel, 1968), 459–65 (p. 465).

[14]   Simon McVeigh, 'The Professional Concert and Rival Subscription Series in London, 1783–1793', *Research Chronicle of the Royal Musical Association*, 22 (1989), 1–136.

[15]   Curtis Price, Judith Milhous and Robert D. Hume, *Italian Opera in Late Eighteenth-Century London*, i: *The King's Theatre, Haymarket, 1778–1791* (Oxford, 1995); Judith Milhous, Gabriella Dideriksen and Robert D. Hume, *Italian Opera in Late Eighteenth-Century London*, ii: *The Pantheon Opera and its Aftermath, 1790–1795* (Oxford, 2001).

[16]   Ian Woodfield, 'John Bland: London Retailer of the Music of Haydn and Mozart', *Music and Letters*, 81 (2000), 210–44.

contain brief accounts of his activities in the 1780s.[17] The star source is undoubtedly Susan Burney, whose diary-letters remain to be edited. Some extracts were published as long ago as 1907, but musicologists have made little use of them yet.[18] Ribeiro, editor of the first volume of Burney's letters, was aware of her writings,[19] but her true significance as a commentator emerged only in the recent study of the King's Theatre for which her journal-letter for 1779–80 (in effect an 'opera diary') was a major source. The authors of this study aptly characterize her as a 'witty and lucid writer, one with good Italian, a technical grasp of music, and an insatiable appetite for rehearsals and backstage gossip'.[20] The journal-letters drawn upon for this study date from around a decade later. They are to be found in the New York Public Library, the British Library and the Armagh Public Library.[21] By then, Susan's circumstances had changed. Married to Captain Phillips with two young children, she lived in idyllic surroundings at Mickleham in Surrey near the River Mole, a short distance from Norbury Park, home of her close friends the Lock family.[22] Susan could now attend opera or concert performances only during her occasional visits to London, but she had lost none of her powers of observation, and in the journal-letters for 1789 and 1790 there are brief but rich descriptions of London concert life on the eve of Haydn's arrival. Through Susan's eyes we witness Salomon's despair at the failure of his 1789 benefit, Giardini's attempts to compose down for his declining powers in 1790, and Giornovichi's very successful first appearance in 1790. When she came to London in the spring of 1791, she chose (alas!) to hear her beloved Pacchierotti at the Pantheon, rather than any of the rival concerts at Hanover Square. The value of the journal-letters from the late 1780s lies above all in her acute observations on domestic music-making and the part played by top professional violinists. Salomon and a Swiss violinist known in England as Scheener were regular visitors at Titchfield Street, home of Esther and Charles Burney, and both men made a more extended summer visit to Mickleham. Susan's reports of the amateur 'concerts' put on with their help are full of pointed observations on the

[17]   British Library, Additional MS 39929; San Marino, Huntington Library, MS HM 54457 (microfilm in the British Library, RP 4744). *The John Marsh Journals: The Life and Times of a Gentleman Composer (1752–1828)*, ed. Brian Robins (Stuyvesant, NY, 1998); British Library, Oriental and India Office Collection, European MS D546/26. See Ian Woodfield, *Music of the Raj: A Social and Economic History of Music in Late Eighteenth-Century Anglo-Indian Society* (Oxford, 2000), 210, 214–17, 222.

[18]   *The House in St Martin's Street: Being Chronicles of the Burney Family*, ed. Mary Constance Hill (London and New York, 1907).

[19]   *The Letters of Charles Burney*, ed. Ribeiro, i.

[20]   Price, Milhous and Hume, *Italian Opera*, i, 23.

[21]   New York Public Library, Berg Collection, Susanna E. B. Phillips, holograph diary for 1786–92; British Library, Egerton MS 3692; journal-letters 1787–95; Armagh Public Library, copies of 27 journal-letters from Susan to Fanny Burney, 1787–8, catalogued as Mrs Molesworth Phillips, Letters, i; copies of 52 journal-letters from Susan to Fanny Burney, 1795–9, catalogued as Mrs Molesworth Phillips, Letters, ii.

[22]   The Duchess of Sermoneta, *The Locks of Norbury* (London, 1940).

refined social and musical etiquette that had to be observed on such occasions.[23] Seemingly inconsequential though these delightful descriptions are, they enable us to study the way in which relationships, developed in the private world of amateur music-making, could influence important public decisions. In the case of Salomon, Susan's letters suggest that, recognizing his public career prospects to be on the wane in London, he attempted to make use of his personal relationship with the family to achieve his as yet unfulfilled ambitions. The reassessment of the early London career of this seminal yet in some ways still enigmatic figure in late eighteenth-century English musical life will clarify the circumstances that led to Haydn's first London visit.

---

[23] On the musical and social organization of private concerts, see Woodfield, *Music of the Raj*, 102–16.

1

Salomon and the Rise of the Professional Concert

Salomon made his début in England on 23 March 1781 in a performance of Arne's *Elfrida*. A review of the performance expresses the sense of slight ambivalence about his playing that was to persist: 'He does not play in the most graceful style, it must be confessed, but his tone and execution are such as cannot fail to secure him a number of admirers in the musical world.'[1] This was a curious inversion of the criticism that was to be made much more commonly – that Salomon could play gracefully but that he lacked the tone and dynamic presence of the true leader. Perhaps a more reliable assessment of the violinist's playing shortly after his arrival in England was that of John Marsh, who played under his direction in a Handel performance at the 1781 Salisbury Music Festival and was unimpressed with his ability as a leader:

19 September 1781

The oratorio of Judas Macchabeus went off very heavily the choruses being very thin & meagre as usual, & the Dead March, w[ch] was introduc'd was very *dead* & dismal indeed; which was principal owing to the unsteadiness of the leader (Salomon who was then not much used to Handel's Music) & of the Double Bass (w[ch] was not Gariboldi this year) who were so far from keeping steadily together that I found the utmost difficulty in beating the Drums, w[ch] when the Extremes were supported by Cramer & Garriboldi, I always found to be perfectly easy.[2]

The perceptive Marsh was not alone in his view that Salomon was not yet a good performer of Handel.[3] On the other hand, the pleasing aspects of Salomon's personality were immediately apparent to everyone. The violinist's good humour when asked to accompany a young child was obvious:

---

[1] *Morning Herald*, 24 March 1781. Cited by Robin Stowell, 'Johann Peter Salomon – Director or Co-ordinator?', *Newsletter of the Haydn Society of Great Britain*, 8 (1988), 8–20 (p. 9).

[2] *The John Marsh Journals*, ed. Robins, 250.

[3] Charlotte Papendiek, *Court and Private Life in the Time of Queen Charlotte: Being the Journals of Mrs Papendiek, Assistant Keeper of the Wardrobe and Reader to her Majesty, Edited by her Grand-Daughter, Mrs Vernon Delves Broughton*, 2 vols. (London, 1887), i, 207, recalled that 'the fondness for the ancient masters kept him [i.e. Salomon] aloof' at the Queen's House, 'much to the annoyance of Abel and Fischer'. Presumably these were the concerts at the Queen's Lodge. See McVeigh, *Concert Life*, 51. Salomon was not involved in the 1784 Handel celebrations.

Immediately on ye conclusion of this Concert a little Boy of the name of Cobham (about 4 Years old, in petticoat) mounted the Orchestra & played one of Borghi's Solos upon the Violin, accomp^d by Mr Salomon, who did it with great good nature.

Salomon's rather impish sense of fun came out in a performance of one of Marsh's own trios:

A concert at Dr Harrington's at which were Salomon, Cervetto, Tenducci, Mahon, Dyne, Short, Miss Guest etc. at the end of which my Trio for a Violin, Tenor, Violoncello was played by Salomon, Myself, Cervetto, the former of whom was so luxurious in his Embellishments that I scarce knew my own piece again. He however did it in great good humour & apologis'd to me for it afterwards.[4]

Another early engagement had been at the Edinburgh Musical Society. The St Cecilia Hall Plan Books show that Salomon appeared in a weekly series of five concerts starting on 29 June. He returned in 1783 for a second series.[5] Early appearances in the provinces formed an important part of the strategy of continental violinists who had ambitions in England. Not even Cramer, the dominant leader in London, could neglect the country 'circuit'. By the late eighteenth century, an annual calendar of festival-style events in the university towns and cathedral cities had developed, providing much-needed summer work. It was worth making an effort to secure such positions. On 11 November 1781, Marsh observed that Salomon, Rauzzini and Tenducci had been 'prevail'd on to come over (to Salisbury) for their expences, or at least on very moderate terms (w'ch they no doubt agreed to with a view to their having a preference at the next Music Festival'.[6] Salomon was indeed invited for the 1782 Salisbury Festival, but thereafter he was replaced by Cramer.[7]

The most extensive account of Salomon's activities in the early 1780s is by Charlotte Papendiek. Her *Journals*, however, are notoriously inaccurate, as they were not written down until 1833, a full 50 years after she first met him. The editor of these journals admits putting the recollections into chronological order, and it is hardly surprising that dates and details of specific performances are thoroughly confused. As a lifelong friend, she recalled Salomon's début in suspiciously eulogistic terms:

The orchestra was, as now, upon the stage, and in due course the concert began. Salomon was to play first, and the desk was brought on, as it still continues to be. Then he appeared, introduced by Abel, Fischer and Mr. Papendiek following. He was not handsome nor of an imposing figure, but the animation of his countenance, and the great elegance of his manner, soon caught the public eye. Having bowed, he so placed the desk that not the smallest particle of his

[4] *The John Marsh Journals*, ed. Robins, 251.
[5] Edinburgh University Library, Special Collections.
[6] *The John Marsh Journals*, ed. Robins, 253.
[7] See Douglas J. Reid and Brian Pritchard, 'Some Festival Programmes of the Eighteenth and Nineteenth Centuries: 1. Salisbury and Winchester', *Research Chronicle of the Royal Musical Association*, 5 (1965), 51–79.

violin was hidden, and the 'Tutti' of his favourite concerto by Kreutzer, commenced rather mezzo-piano, and increased to a crescendo that drew down volumes of applause. Now came the solo; a repetition of the melody an octave higher, which he played with an effect perfectly sublime. It was in the minor key, and the cadence he introduced was a long shake, with the melody played under – something new, which put Fischer almost into fits. The adagio movement he performed in such a manner that Fischer was heard to say, 'I will play it no more; he has outdone me.' Then the rondo followed in the same key as the first movement, and Salomon introduced one short variation that struck upon the ear in such a manner that it was difficult to keep quiet. Having finished, he returned his instrument to the attendant, but retained the bow, which assisted his gracious bow. Abel, who had been permitted to sit, now rose, and they went off arm in arm. Such a *début* has scarcely ever been experienced. We were jumping from our seats.[8]

The friendship that developed was a lasting one.[9] Mrs Papendiek remembered Salomon as a very congenial visitor, who often took his 'two o'clock meal' at her house and on one occasion slept overnight 'to enjoy his coffee breakfast, to have his shoe buckled and his cravat tied'.[10] Her journals give a pleasant if doubtless idealized picture of an urbane and successful society musician.

Salomon's quest for a top position as an orchestral leader coincided with a major reorganization in the patterns of concert-giving in London. McVeigh's research has clarified the transition between the Bach–Abel concert series, the dominant force in the 1770s, and the Professional Concert, which emerged to occupy a position of similar eminence in the later 1780s.[11] The precise role of Salomon in these changes has remained elusive, and his relationship with Cramer during the formative years

[8] Papendiek, *Court and Private Life*, i, 185–7. This performance is described as though it were the 1783 Concert for the New Musical Fund, although if it took place in 1783 it would have been for the Decayed Musicians' Fund. The details of the programme, however, do not equate to the published programme for this concert (or any other). It is therefore probably a muddled conflation of several public and perhaps private concerts. Some of the details of concert etiquette are interesting: the positioning of the music stand; the handing of the violin to an attendant to facilitate an elegant bow.

[9] In one passage, Papendiek exclaims effusively: 'Dear friend, we appreciated, we respected, we loved you! Farewell to thy memory.' Papendiek, *Court and Private Life*, i, 192.

[10] *Ibid.*, 207, 330.

[11] McVeigh, 'The Professional Concert'. The impressive effect of a Bach–Abel concert is captured by Edward Piggot in his diary for April 1776, New Haven, Yale University, Beinecke Library, Osborn, f.c. 80: 'April the 16th, 1776 Lord Fauconbery sent me a ticket for Bach and Abels Concert at the Assembly room in Hanover Square the performers were the two above mentioned, the second play[ed] a solo exceeding well; the others were Giardini, [Crosdill crossed out] who plays on the Violin supprising well is Cramer; Crosdill on the Violoncello plays exceeding well, Fischer on the hautboy the same, all Capital performer[s], Savoi, Grassi, & several other[s] sang; Signora Grassi has a supprising Voice being a tenor, which is very singular and I thing [think] disagreable. In all about 22 musicians; this concert is rec[k]oned the best in the world, every thing executed with the greatest teast [taste] and exactness; a very fine room 115 feet long 40 broad; very elegantly painted; it was almost full, every body Dressed; between the acts they go in another room under neigh [neath] w[h]ere you have tea; it is by subscription; it begins at about 8 and end[s] at 10 every thing is very elegant.'

between 1783 and 1785 is especially hard to fathom. During his first two seasons in London, Salomon's public appearances had been confined largely to benefits. Referring to the period before July 1784 (when Giardini left England), Papendiek recalled that Salomon did not yet enjoy as prominent a public role as his two rivals: 'he [Salomon] was generally engaged for the private concerts, Giardini having the Opera, and Cramer the established concerts'.[12] In 1783 Salomon achieved his first break-through when he was invited to join the Earl of Abingdon's Hanover Square Grand Concert. Although Cramer was leader, Salomon played a prominent part in the season's programmes, performing three violin concertos and playing the solo viola in concertante works. This arrangement came briefly into question when a rival series at the Free-masons' Hall was announced. At first Cramer was advertised as leader, but the principal performers from Hanover Square were forbidden to take part, and in the event Salomon (who presumably placed his position at Hanover Square in jeopardy to do so) led the only concert to take place. Whether, as implied by one writer, there was any friction between the two men as a result of this venture is unclear, but it seems unlikely, because after this brief interruption Salomon returned as an active member of Abingdon's orchestra for the remainder of the season.[13]

There can be little doubt that Salomon was actively seeking to establish himself independently of Cramer, because at the end of the season he decided to look elsewhere for a more substantial role for himself. The most important project under consideration in the summer of 1783 was a plan to recruit Haydn to the King's Theatre as an opera composer. Abingdon's attempt to attract the composer to England for his concert series early in 1783 had ended in failure, but the publicity set others thinking. Burney, who was constantly on the lookout for ways of enriching Italian opera in London, suggested to Gallini the possibility of recruiting Haydn as house composer. In a letter to Thomas Twining dated 6 September 1783, he expressed alarm that the machinations at the opera house (where the new manager was striving to establish himself) might jeopardize the project: 'I have stimulated a wish to get Haydn over as opera Composer – but mum mum – yet – a correspondence is opened, & there is a great likelihood of it, if these Cabals, & litigations ruin not the opera entirely.'[14] On 12 November,

---

[12] Papendiek, *Court and Private Life*, i, 207.

[13] McVeigh, 'The Professional Concert', 27.

[14] *The Letters of Charles Burney*, ed. Ribeiro, i, 382, cites Burney's MS 'Materials Towards the History of German Music and Musicians': 'He [Haydn] was engaged to Compose for Ld Abingdon's Concert and was expected in England ab^t the end of the year 1782; but did not come, as the security for his money: (£300, & travelling expenses from Vienna; & at the end of the Season £100 more for Copy-right, of the 12 Pieces he was to compose for the concert, of whatever kind he pleased, if he c^d not dispose of them more to his advantage.)' Haydn had apparently been ready to travel to England, but 'a certain circumstance' had hindered the plan. Landon, *Haydn at Esterháza*, 477. On this first attempt to recruit Haydn to England, see Roscoe, 'Haydn and London', 203–5. On Abingdon's later contacts with Haydn, see H. C. Robbins Landon, 'Haydn und die Familie Bertie', *Österreichische Musik Zeitschrift*, 43 (1988), 21–4.

Burney informed Twining that he had seen a letter from Haydn in response to the proposal:

Did I tell you that Gallini's agents shewed me a Letter from Haydn, in wch he was in treaty to come over for the opera – all is in such Confusion now that there remains no hope for this Winter – but – who knows, when I have mounted my *Ballon*, but he may yet come?[15]

An announcement in the *General Advertiser* on 9 July 1783 suggests that Salomon was aware of these negotiations and could even have been party to them himself.[16] His proposal was for a series of 12 concerts at Willis's Rooms to begin in February 1784, with Haydn as composer:

The Concerts, at Willis's room in King-street, are fixed for February next, and as his Royal Highness the Prince of Wales and most of the first Nobility are patrons of this select assembly, the music is the best that ever yet has appeared in London; Mr. Hayden the highly celebrated composer from Italy, with many of the principal performers, vocal and instrumental, in that country, are engaged. There are to be, it seems, but twelve nights, and the subscription, which is limited to a certain number of persons, is near complete already. Saloman [*sic*] plays the first violin and leads the band, and has the conduct of the orchestra.

By making reference to the patronage of the Prince of Wales, Salomon was implying that he had made progress at the highest levels of society, and there is some independent confirmation of this. In Cramer's *Magazin der Musik* (30 May 1783) it was reported that 'the celebrated violinist Herr Salomon recently played before their Majesties by express command and received extraordinary approbation'.[17]

What is significant about Salomon's announcement is that it coincided exactly with Gallini's interest in Haydn. The opera impresario finally reached agreement to take over the King's Theatre on 5 June, and on 21 June he formally agreed to accept responsibility for all debts. As Price, Milhous and Hume argue, he 'quite reasonably presumed that he was now duly in possession, and set about laying plans for the season of 1783–4'.[18] His first trip, made some time between mid-June and mid-July, was to Paris, to recruit Vestris and a team of dancers, and then around 20 July he set off for Italy, not returning until early November. The first report of Gallini's activities comes in the *Morning Herald* of 19 July in a piece which reports as a *fait accompli* Haydn's proposed visit:

Hayden, next autumn, comes to London. Extreme caution, are among the leading characteristics of this great composer, insomuch so, that last Winter he

15 *The Letters of Charles Burney*, ed. Ribeiro, i, 401.
16 McVeigh, 'The Professional Concert', 32.
17 Cramer, *Magazin der Musik*, i/2, 828 (London, 30 May 1783): 'Der berühmte Violinist Herr Salomon, spielte neulich vor Ihro Majestäten durch ausdrücklichen Verlangen und erhielt ausserordentlich Beyfall.'
18 Price, Milhous and Hume, *Italian Opera*, i, 74.

could not, without uncommon assurances, be prevailed on to send his new music over to Lord Abingdon's Grand Concert.[19]

The reference to 'autumn' relates to the proposal to hire Haydn for the King's Theatre – for a subscription series he would not have been needed until the new year. Although reported to Twining only in September, Burney's suggestion that Gallini should try to recruit Haydn as his opera composer may therefore be dated to the period around the end of June. It was entirely characteristic of Burney to make an effort to establish a relationship of influence with any new management at the King's Theatre. He had done so with Brooke in 1773 and again when Sheridan took over.[20] What is not so clear is the extent to which Burney knew of Haydn as an opera composer. When informing Twining of Pacchierotti's arrival on 12 November 1783, he wrote: 'I have made him very fond of a Cantat[a] by Haydn, lately come from Vienna, "Ah, come il core mi palpita" – It is so much in his best style of singing that it seems *fatta apposta per lui*.'[21] The 'cantata' was in fact a *scena* from Act 2 of Haydn's opera *La fedeltà premiata*, published as a cantata by Artaria in Vienna in 1783.[22] If Burney was in possession of Artaria's print or a manuscript copy by early June, his recommendation to Gallini would have been made with specific and recent knowledge of Haydn's operatic style.

The timing of Salomon's announcement on 9 July suggests that a joint venture could have been under discussion between Gallini and himself, an agreement to offer Haydn both an opera commission and a concert series. If so, this was the first appearance of the oft-repeated package that the composer finally accepted in 1790. Salomon's confident announcement of a nearly full subscription, the patronage of the Prince of Wales, and the successful recruitment of Haydn and the principal Italian singers was doubtless mere kite-flying, but even as a piece of speculation the notice had one immediate practical purpose: to inform the public of his intention to trump Cramer and Abingdon, who had just failed in the first attempt to lure Haydn to England. Nothing in Salomon's character suggests that he was in any way a mean-spirited or vindictive individual, but professionally he was clearly a competitive man for whom playing the viola to Cramer's violin was not enough. From this moment, the rivalry between the two men was pointed, and at times perhaps even sharp, although it was never a bitter, personal

---

[19]   The report also appeared in the *Morning Post* on 19 July. The text began: 'The great Hayden, next autumn, comes to London. Phlegm, and, in all pecuniary concerns, extreme caution ...'. The *Morning Herald* on 22 July reported further: 'Mr Gallini has hitherto been indefatigable. He has been already once in France, for the purpose of engaging Vestris, who is certainly engaged. He returned to London on business, and now is again gone to the Continent.'
[20]   Ian Woodfield, *Opera and Drama in Eighteenth-Century London: The King's Theatre, Garrick and the Business of Performance* (Cambridge, 2001), 52–3; Price, Milhous and Hume, *Italian Opera*, i, 183–4.
[21]   *The Letters of Charles Burney*, ed. Ribeiro, i, 398.
[22]   Copy in London, British Library, E409.cc.

quarrel, as is shown by occasional invitations to Salomon to perform at the Professional Concert. Salomon's initiative came to nothing, as Haydn refused to come. In Cramer's *Magazin* (December 1783) it was reported that 'Hayden's intention, of which I wrote you recently, to come here has turned out to amount to nothing. He has categorically turned down our offer but promised to compose anything we wish if he receives the sum of £500.'[23] One year later, Burney was still expressing disappointment over the failure of this plan. He wrote on 9 November 1784 to Sir Robert Murray Keith, the British envoy in Vienna:

I had last year hopes that the admirable Haydn the chief ornament of the Vienna School & of the Age, w^d have made us a visit; If the universal admiration & performance of his works w^d be a temptation to visit us, I can as[s]ure him of that claim to his favour; but as to the opera, at present, its regency is in such confusion that it is hardly certain whether its existence will be ascertained during the ensuing Winter.[24]

The events of July 1783 had no immediate result, but they set the scene for the next decade. The politics of the London musical world now entered a period of exceptional turbulence. Gallini's hopes of assuming complete control of the King's Theatre were thwarted, and the affairs of the opera house fell into a state of chaos. Cramer, meanwhile, after one further season with Abingdon, founded the Professional Concert, which, partly as a result of its increasingly close alliance with Gallini, soon developed into London's leading orchestra. Salomon did not take part in Abingdon's final series, nor was he asked to join the Professional Concert in 1785. Busby, a later source, believed that he had been 'piqued' at his 'exclusion'.[25]

In furtherance of his ambitions, Salomon now aligned himself with the Pantheon, where he was appointed leader of a short series in 1784, perhaps at the behest of Burney, who seems also to have had some role in securing the services of Mara. In a letter to him dated 12 November 1783, Mara wrote that she had just refused an offer from Gallini of £1,200, on the grounds that she did not believe that she could perform [in concerts] twice a week during the opera season.[26] The letter does not make clear what the two performances a week were, but it seems likely that Gallini had offered her a dual contract (of the kind that later became standard during his management) to perform both in *opera seria* and in a concert series at Hanover Square. Mara's refusal and the failure

---

[23]   Landon, *Haydn at Esterháza*, 596.

[24]   *The Letters of Charles Burney*, ed. Ribeiro, i, 448.

[25]   Thomas Busby, *Concert Room and Orchestra: Anecdotes of Music and Musicians, Ancient and Modern*, 3 vols., (London, 1825), ii, 142: 'Piqued at not being included in the "Professional Concert", and hearing that Haydn had been engaged by Lord Abingdon, and that the great composer had been disappointed by the termination of his Lordship's management, Salomon went to Germany, and brought him to London.' This is a rather naive and highly abbreviated version of the decade-long campaign to bring Haydn to London.

[26]   McVeigh, 'The Professional Concert', 36. The full text of Mara's letter to Burney is given in Price, Milhous and Hume, *Italian Opera*, i, 300–2.

of Abel to contact her about his proposed series (which never took place) left her in need of an engagement, and it is reasonable to suppose that Burney made her an offer on behalf of the Pantheon.[27] The short series seems to have been financially unsuccessful. There were reports of poor audiences.[28] Papendiek recalled the scene as Salomon introduced Mara, though the description appears to be confused with a similar occasion in his 1786 series.[29]

The 1785 season was dominated by the competition between Cramer's newly founded Professional Concert at Hanover Square and the Pantheon Grand Concert, which again featured Mara, with Salomon as leader.[30] But whereas the Professional Concert seems to have made at least a small profit, the Pantheon season lost, according to some reports, £1,200.[31] Unequal though the financial outcome may have been, this season was the only occasion before 1791 in which Salomon and Cramer competed on reasonably equal terms, both staging a series of 12 concerts.

The summer of 1785 was perhaps the last time during the decade when Cramer and Salomon could have been viewed as equals. Salomon was hired for the prestigious Oxford Commemoration of Founders and Benefactors to the University.[32] By chance, Twining heard both violinists at Cambridge. In his first letter to Burney on the subject, he expresses warm appreciation of Salomon's playing at Cramer's expense:

Fordham 16 June 1785   Thomas Twining to Charles Burney

I heard Salomon too, whom I had not heard before. I like him very much better than Cramer. Cramer is very goo[d at] mechanism. Salomon played as many hard tricks as the lover of difficulty could wish; but with more appearance of taste, I think – more tone, more glow, more symptoms of feeling than Cramer. With my eyes shut I could tell that the fiddle was played by a human creature.

By the autumn, however, he had modified his views:

Fordham 16 September 1785   Thomas Twining to Charles Burney

We had Cramer & Cervetto. Surely Cramer is much improved since I had heard him! – in tone, in fancy, taste etc? I still believe that were I to hear Salomon & Cramer play Quartettos of Haydn, tour à tour, in a room, I sh^d prefer Salomon. But I beg to swallow part of the unjust contempt that I expressed for Cramer in

27   McVeigh, 'The Professional Concert', 37.
28   *Ibid.*, 36. Burney, *A General History*, ed. Mercer, ii, 893, explained the failure as follows: 'The dissolution of parliament and general election happening so soon after her arrival, the audiences to which she sung were not very numerous.'
29   Papendiek, *Court and Private Life*, i, 215–16.
30   McVeigh, 'The Professional Concert', 45. According to the *London Magazine*, 4 (1785), 222, Salomon was influential in the choice of repertoire.
31   McVeigh, 'The Professional Concert', 44.
32   I am grateful to Charles Mould for checking the reference in *Jackson's Oxford Journal*, 18 June 1785.

my last letter. I did not do him justice. He is [a mas]terly player, & has *more* soul & energy than he used to have: is it not so?[33]

In Burney circles, Salomon usually received warm approbation for his quiet musicality, even over the brilliant and dynamic playing of Cramer. When making his definitive appraisal of the two men in the closing pages of his *General History of Music*, Burney opted diplomatically for a neutral tone, contrasting the 'fire, tone, and certainty of a Cramer' with the 'taste, refinement, and enthusiasm of a Salomon'.[34] But behind the generally positive tone of these appraisals lay the shadow of the persistent criticism that his playing was not dynamic enough in the context of orchestral leadership to match that of Cramer.

If there was a measure of equality in the public reputations of the two men, it was to be short-lived, for the 1786 season saw Cramer's dominance established beyond question. The key event was Gallini's final defeat of Taylor's trustees in the agreement signed on 14 September 1785. It is surely no coincidence that a mere two days after this accord was agreed, the *Gazetteer* should have alluded to speculation about a possible Haydn visit: 'The report of the celebrated *Haydn's* intention of visiting this country, is again revived. Those however, who know him best, are of the opinion, that he will never honor this land of *heresy* with his presence.'[35] Apart from a bizarre suggestion earlier in the year that Haydn should be kidnapped, this was the first time that a visit had been mentioned since Gallini's earlier attempt. It was of course far too late for the forthcoming opera season, and on 2 November the *Gazetteer* confirmed its earlier suspicions that the composer would not be coming. But Cramer's rise stemmed not from wishful thinking about Haydn, but from an understanding he had reached with Gallini which was to have far-reaching consequences. At the heart of this concordat were the controversial contracts offered to (or perhaps forced upon) his star singers, which obliged them to perform at Hanover Square.[36] This mutually beneficial arrangement had some characteristics of a cartel, with Cramer holding a joint appointment as leader of the opera orchestra and as impresario and leader of the subscription series, and Gallini exercising an influential dual role as opera impresario and proprietor of the concert room. The financial details of these interlocking agreements, which McVeigh went as far as to describe as 'shady dealing', remain unclear, but Gallini's enemies at the King's Theatre were furious, claiming with some justification that he was subsidizing Hanover Square by providing the Professional Concert

---

[33]   British Library, Additional MS 39929.

[34]   Burney, *A General History*, ed. Mercer, ii, 1021.

[35]   Roscoe, 'Haydn and London', 206.

[36]   Price, Milhous and Hume, *Italian Opera*, i, 337–8. See also Judith Milhous and Robert D. Hume, 'Opera Salaries in Eighteenth-Century London', *Journal of the American Musicological Society*, 46 (1993), 26–83.

with some of the finest singers in Europe.[37] The opportunity of presenting castrati of the calibre of Rubinelli in 1787 and Marchesi in 1788 at below their market fees gave the Professional Concert a considerable financial advantage over any other promoter, a not-so-hidden subsidy that in significant measure enhanced the deserved success the organization enjoyed in the second half of the 1780s for its orchestral playing.[38]

The potential loser in all this was the rival series at the Pantheon. Its star singer, Mara, was a very tough-minded individual, and she now set about negotiating a deal on her own terms. Gallini, having taken over only in September 1785, was in urgent need of star singers, but when he wrote to Lord Cowper on 20 September, he asked only about a *primo uomo* and a *primo buffo*, commenting that he would recruit the other singers from those 'remaining in London'.[39] Almost certainly he had Mara in mind as *prima donna seria*, but again she resolutely refused to sign a double contract. This automatically placed her in conflict with the Professional Concert, and a dispute broke out. First it was reported that Cramer's orchestra had offered her an engagement for £500.[40] Possibly as a bargaining ploy, she announced plans for her own concert series in direct competition with the Professionals. A furious press row erupted, in which a strongly xenophobic tone is evident. One report claimed that Mara's orchestra was 'not to contain one Englishman'.[41] Several weeks later, the same paper commented that the ire of the 'British Lion' had been aroused and was not easily to be quelled. Mara's behaviour in attempting to set up her own subscription 'merely for the power of exercising that contempt with which she has ever treated the English' was deplored.[42] When the subscription failed, Mara claimed that she had not in fact been approached by the Professional Concert and would have agreed if she had been. In the end, the singer apparently got her way; Gallini signed her up for £800 for the abbreviated 1785–6 opera season and for £1,200 for the following year. Alone of all the leading singers, her contract did not include the requirement to sing at Hanover Square.[43] It has been necessary to look in detail at Mara's negotiations with Gallini, because the result compounded a serious setback for Salomon. Having ended the 1785 season substantially out of pocket, the Pantheon management was apparently reluctant to risk further losses with the current team of performers. Since Mara, the one singer with enough of a reputation to attract an economic audience, was about to join the cast at the King's

---

[37] McVeigh, *Concert Life*, 171–2.
[38] It should be borne in mind that the finances of the top subscription series were balanced on a knife edge, and there was no certainty at all of even a modest profit. *Ibid.*, 167–73.
[39] Price, Milhous and Hume, *Italian Opera*, i, 341.
[40] McVeigh, 'The Professional Concert', 50.
[41] *Morning Post*, 1 November 1785.
[42] *Ibid.*, 23 November 1785.
[43] Milhous and Hume, 'Opera Salaries', 50.

Theatre and was seemingly unwilling to take on a full subscription series as well, the only option open to Salomon seems to have been to advertise at his own risk a short series of four concerts at the Pantheon.

The role of planted 'puffs' in building an audience for a concert series is well known. Apart from items actually written by the performers themselves, it was often possible to influence other reviewers, especially if they had no intention of attending the concert![44] A good example of systematic puffing is the sequence of reviews of Salomon's four concerts in the *General Advertiser*. The first performance was reported to have been attended 'by a brilliant train of subscribers', a characteristic selling-point. The music was not bad either! The overture by Mozart had been 'a grand composition and was executed with great spirit and effect'. Salomon's concerto had been performed 'with such force, precision, and expression, as demonstrated the full power of the instrument, and justly procured a profusion of plaudits'.[45] Puffs did not always consist of unfocused and effusive flattery; often the wording suggests an attempt to present a rebuttal of a known criticism – in this case the niggling complaint that Salomon did not make use of 'the full power' of the instrument. The following week's concert was reported to have been 'graced by a very numerous auditory'. Making increasing use of superlatives, the reviewer noted that Salomon 'appeared to derive unusual animation from the general excellence of the performers, and plaudits of the company'; he reached 'such a brilliancy of execution' as had never before been heard from him. Typically for a puff, there was now a forecast, which demonstrates a clear awareness of the competitive context of the rival subscriptions. Salomon's series, it was claimed, 'bids fair to become a principal favourite with the *cognoscenti*, amidst all the various rivals'.[46] And so it continued. In the report of the third concert, there was even some comment on the music: 'The Overture by Haydn, was a charming piece, abounding in all the wild graces of that admirable composer.'[47] The final review expressed the wish 'that the conductor may comply with the general desire of having two more of these delicious evenings before the termination of the season'.[48] Apparently unconvinced by his own publicity, Salomon did not extend the season. Evidently the prospects were not as rosy as claimed.

During the course of the 1786 season, Cramer and the Professional Concert sought to establish their position further by developing an agreement with Haydn to supply them with music. An item in the press

[44] McVeigh, 'The Professional Concert', 17, cites a letter published in 1784 which claims that reviews were often written by 'needy scribblers' who rarely passed the threshold where concerts were held but stopped performers at the door to find out details of the programme. The writer claimed that the practice was especially prevalent at Hanover Square.
[45] *General Advertiser*, 3 March 1786.
[46] *Ibid.*, 11 March 1786.
[47] *Ibid.*, 17 March 1786.
[48] *Ibid.*, 24 March 1786.

the previous year had suggested that several Haydn manuscripts had been received.[49] Now there were renewed and seemingly authoritative claims. The *Public Advertiser* on 8 October 1785 reported: 'He [Haydn] certainly undertakes to write for the Hanover-square concert; his genius is yet in its full vigour; and what may we not expect from its exertions, if we may judge from what we have already experienced?'[50] The composer's good wishes were even reported in the *Morning Herald* on 6 February 1786, the opening night of the season: 'Haydn wishes it [the Professional Concert] prosperity, and has composed some pieces that will be played there, full of his phrenzy and fire.' The campaign gathered momentum as preparations for the 1787 season got under way, and by late 1786 there was intense speculation in the press about a contract for the composer to visit London in January to compose for the Hanover Square concert series. His imminent arrival was predicted.[51] Gallini again synchronized his own efforts. He let it be known that he hoped to recruit Haydn as an opera composer. A report in the *Morning Chronicle* on 10 October 1786 stated:

Gallini is now at Vienna for the express purpose of engaging the celebrated Haydn, as composer to the Opera House for the ensuing season. Should he succeed, the King's Theatre will be in possession of more musical excellence than any other in Europe.[52]

The composer's rejection of Gallini's latest offer was reported in the *Morning Post* on 30 December 1786:

To the great regret of the musical world, it is now certain that *Haydn* will not visit this country, whatever may be conceived by the hopes of some, or propagated by the *policy* of others. As a proof that he never intended to come, notwithstanding the sanguine assertions which have so frequently been given to the public on this head, it is positively true, that the manager of the Opera House wrote to this celebrated composer, to desire him to come to England, in order to make an opera; but the answer from *Haydn* was, that he was very willing to compose an opera, and would send a confidential substitute to conduct the performance; but as to himself, he could never think of undertaking such a journey.

This reported offer to send a substitute to direct a performance of a new opera might be seen as a reflection of the composer's desire to build his reputation in London, even though he could not leave his current employment. Yet the author of this piece was obviously a sceptic of the plan to recruit Haydn, and the veracity of the information must remain somewhat suspect. The charge that Gallini, Cramer and the

---

49 McVeigh, 'The Professional Concert', 39.
50 Roscoe, 'Haydn and London', 206.
51 *Ibid.*, 207.
52 *Ibid.*, 206. This report is contradicted by the evidence of Stephen Storace, who later testified that he had met Gallini in London in September 1786, shortly before his own departure for Vienna. Price, Milhous and Hume, *Italian Opera*, i, 362. Whether Storace had remembered the date correctly is now impossible to establish.

Professional Concert were engaging in a publicity campaign, raising ill-founded hopes of a Haydn visit for their own ends, was one that would surface again.

In July 1787, Gallini made his by now routine proposal to hire Haydn, and for once some documentary evidence survives. On 8 April 1787, Haydn had written to William Forster, the London music publisher, that he hoped to see him personally at the end of the year. He complained that he had not yet heard from Cramer and hinted that he intended to accept an engagement in Naples.[53] The composer's reply to Gallini dated 19 July is known only from an English translation in Sotheby's auction catalogue of 2 March 1905. It begins rather cryptically, at least in the English version: 'I acknowledge to have received your letter dated the 26th of last June and then, when I thought to have heard of your offers, you request once more to know my terms.'[54] The chronology of this unclear. It is conceivable that by 'last' June Haydn could have meant June 1786, which would confirm that Gallini had at least contacted Haydn by post the previous summer, but if, as seems much more probable, Haydn was responding to a more recent approach, the timetable of events was as follows:

7 June	Gallini writes to Cowper to tell him that he intends to travel to Italy himself to recruit singers. He hopes to be in Florence in July.[55]
18 June	Gallini writes to Andrea Campigli (who has been negotiating on his behalf with Marchesi) to say that as soon as the opera season is over he will leave for Italy.
26 June	Gallini writes again to Cowper to say that he has sent a letter to Campigli and that he intends to leave for Italy early in July.[56]
26 June	Gallini writes to Haydn asking for his terms.[57]
6 July	Gallini leaves for Italy.[58]
12–16 July	Gallini, en route to Italy, sends Haydn another letter asking for his terms.
19 July	Haydn, slightly taken aback by the receipt of two letters in quick succession, replies to Gallini in London.

This tight schedule, with duplicate letters being posted in quick succession, is not at all untypical of the way in which opera casts were

---

[53] Landon, *Haydn at Esterháza*, 691. Joseph Haydn, *Gesammelte Briefe und Aufzeichnungen*, ed. H. C. Robbins Landon and Dénes Bartha (Kassel, 1965), 163: 'Ich verhoffe Sie zu Ende dieses Jahres selbst zu sehen.'
[54] Haydn, *Briefe*, ed. Landon and Bartha, 173.
[55] Elizabeth Gibson, 'Earl Cowper in Florence and his Correspondence with the Italian Opera in London', *Music and Letters*, 67 (1987), 235–52 (p. 247).
[56] *Ibid.*, 248.
[57] Haydn, *Briefe*, ed. Landon and Bartha, 173.
[58] The final performance of the 1786–7 season at the King's Theatre was on 5 July.

recruited. Haydn offered two alternatives for a contract, one of which would have involved him in a dual arrangement with Cramer. He asked for £500 plus a benefit for a contract with Gallini alone, but for £500 plus two benefits if hired jointly by Gallini and Cramer.[59]

Reviewing all the evidence of the way in which the careers of the two violinists were developing, it seems clear that between 1785 and 1787 Salomon was comprehensively out-manoeuvred by his rival. Against the growing commercial and artistic dominance of the Professional Concert and its strengthening links with Haydn, he could offer only the short series at the Pantheon, managed by himself in 1786 and by Mara in 1787. The celebrated quarrel that flared up between Haydn and the Professional Concert in the spring of 1788 was perhaps the first sign that Cramer was not invulnerable. Yet while this débâcle undoubtedly gave Salomon a long-term edge in the competition to win Haydn's services, there was little immediate tactical gain for him. Above all, what comes across clearly from the first phase of the struggle between the two violinists is the extent to which Gallini was the driving force behind attempts to recruit Haydn. Within days of taking control (as he thought) in 1783, the plan to approach Haydn with an offer was under discussion; two days after his assumption of full control in September 1785, the press was speculating about the revival of the plan; in 1786 there is an unconfirmed report of a direct approach to the composer; and then in 1787 there is documentary proof of one.

[59] Landon, *Haydn at Esterháza*, 696. The wording of Haydn's letter suggests that Gallini had offered him a contract to compose an opera and symphonies *with or without* Cramer. If the proposed contract was to be with Gallini alone, Haydn agreed to 'assist' at his [i.e. Gallini's] concerts in Hanover Square. Assuming that this was not a simple misunderstanding on the composer's part of the relationship between Gallini and Cramer, it implies that Gallini was willing to countenance a rival series of concerts at Hanover Square. Gallini perhaps regarded Haydn as so valuable an asset that he was willing, if necessary, to break with Cramer, albeit still allowing him the use of Hanover Square.

2

The Country Visit

While Salomon was less in demand than Cramer as a leader of 'public' concerts because of his lack of assertiveness, his qualities as a top chamber player and in particular as a fine leader of quartets were never doubted.[1] As one writer put it, 'his style was not bold enough for the orchestra, but it was exquisite in a quartett'.[2] In the later 1780s, relatively lean years when he was very much in Cramer's shadow as an orchestral leader, Salomon had to rely increasingly on private engagements to make his living. In effect, he had to develop an alternative career as what might be termed a 'society' violinist.

The musical characteristics which a violinist active in the private sphere was expected to possess reflected the social setting. With characteristic insight, Susan Burney commented on the question in the account of her first meeting with a Swiss violinist named Scheener during his visit to her sister Esther's home in the summer of 1787. Her preference for this kind of player is quite clear:

We should certainly have gone [to the theatre] had there not been an uncertain expectation of M. Schinar [Scheener], a *violinist*, who has been some time in Dublin, but who is yet scarce known here, with whom our cousins were delighted & who had half promised them to come that evening – He kept his word, & arrived whilst we were at tea. He is a tall, gentlemanlike looking young man – of very quiet & modest manners – by birth a Swiss – he reminded me in his manner a little, at times, of Pacchierotti. The evening was given to music, & it was deliciously spent to me . . . In Schinar is an exquisite player – in a room it is impossible to be more sweet, more delicate, more perfect – the nearer you are to him indeed the better – for there is never a rough tone, or a note out of tune, or any defect – in a Theatre perhaps his tone would not be sufficiently powerful, but were I a gentleman I had rather play like Schinar than any other of the many great & admirable players I have heard.[3]

Good breeding, refinement and smoothness of tone rather than power were the qualities most prized in a society chamber violinist. Marsh, who heard Scheener in a concert at Salisbury in May 1782, concurred with Susan Burney that he was too weak to make a successful leader:

---

[1]   One reviewer, for example, whilst describing him as a genius, commented that his performance of an unidentified solo was 'perhaps not excelling in tone'. Landon, *Haydn in England*, 25.

[2]   William Gardiner, *Music and Friends*, 2 vols. (London, 1838), i, 356. Cited in McVeigh, *The Violinist*, 115.

[3]   Armagh Public Library, copies of 27 journal-letters from Susan to Fanny Burney, 1787–8, Letter xiii, p. 136, 6 August 1787.

Mr Shanere (who play'd 2nd fiddle to Mr Pieltain lately at Bath) to lead the Concert. I . . . went to meet him . . . & try over some music for the Concert the next day, when I found him to be a very good player, but rather weak as a leader owing to a complaint in his wrist . . . The next day I went to the Concert, which Mr Shanere (now called Scheener) led.[4]

In much the same way that leading violinists vied for the top public positions, there was parallel competition in the private sphere for access to influential patrons. It was of course an altogether more fluid struggle for influence, with fewer outright winners and with opportunities for those who could not quite make it in the public domain as soloists or leaders to thrive. It is clear too that the development of a useful private connection could pose many a practical dilemma for the professional. Because the laws of supply and demand were so seasonal, a violinist might one week be anxious for work of any kind, while the next he might have to exercise self-interest as diplomatically as possible in deciding to take up a public engagement rather than the offer of private work.

During the season in London, there was great demand for professional violinists at private musical soirées, but in the summer months, as large numbers left for their country residences, this type of work tailed off. Instead, extended visits to the country were on offer from keen amateur musicians, anxious to enrich what otherwise might have seemed a rather impoverished diet of music-making with family and friends. Securing the services of a violinist of sufficient ability to ensure high-quality music became for many a matter of urgent concern. For their part, professional musicians seem to have been very happy to accept such engagements, perhaps because of their potential in helping to build a loyal audience for the next season. In the case of members of the Burney family, who exerted considerable indirect influence on the politics of the London concert world, there was the additional possibility of winning valuable support in the quest for major leaderships in the metropolis.

The social, musical and financial dimensions of the country visit have been little investigated. It is far from clear, for example, whether a weekend spent in a rural residence was regarded as a professional engagement (attracting a fee) or whether it was an extension of the 'bread-and-butter' principle described by Parke, in which hospitality, the possibility of further engagements, and support at a benefit were understood to be the rewards.[5] Payments were doubtless given for

---

[4]   *The John Marsh Journals*, ed. Robins, 265. The initial uncertainty over the spelling of Scheener's German name (Schöner or Schüner) persisted. Susan Burney changed from Schinar in 1787 to Scheener in 1788. Burney gave the name as Schoener: *A General History*, ed. Mercer, ii, 1021. As Marsh reports, the confusion was apparently compounded by a name change: 'Mr Shanere (now called Sheener) led.'

[5]   William T. Parke, *Musical Memoirs*, 2 vols. (London, 1830), ii, 16–17. Salomon was a noted exponent of the 'bread-and-butter' concert party: 'That these concerts [Salomon's subscription series in 1808] were not well attended was rather surprising, as Salomon's

many private performances, but such was Burney's influence in the musical world that musicians probably played for members of his family without charge. To be a success in the elegant world of the country home, a professional musician needed to master the social graces. If anything, correct social deportment was even more important than musical proficiency. To flatter one's hosts without becoming embarrassingly obsequious, to promote one's own abilities and importance without seeming arrogant, required a sensitive touch.

In the late 1780s, the intensely musical households of the Burney daughters played host to two of the suavest society violinists, Scheener and Salomon, both apparently intent on developing their influence. Susan Burney recorded a substantial set-piece description of a weekend visit from each of the two, accounts which provide charming insights into the social and musical behaviour adopted during the summer country visit, arguably one of the most vital intersections between the worlds of the amateur and professional musician in late eighteenth-century England.

To set the scene for Salomon's visit in 1789, we shall examine the position in the Burney households established by Scheener in 1788, first during an extended country visit, then, as virtual professional-in-residence, during the early months of the 1789 London season. When Salomon made his pitch with the family in the autumn of that year, he was setting himself up for comparison with a very skilled 'society' player, whose manners and musicianship had utterly beguiled Susan Burney.

The good first impression made by Scheener on the Burneys led to repeated requests from Captain Phillips for a visit to his country home. The musician had promised to come in the spring, and the explanation for his failure to do so was that he had been 'called to a sick friend Mr Pfeiffer, who is in Hereford', where he had remained two months.[6] Now, however, he was available to visit. For a 'society' violinist on a country visit, the presence of children represented a challenge and an opportunity. On this occasion, there was a small tribe of young Burneys: Susan's two children, Frances ('Fanny') aged about six and [Charles] Norbury ('Nordia') aged about three, and her cousin Charles Rousseau Burney (who had married her sister Esther) and his brother Edward, a young artist. William and Frederica Augusta Lock, who resided nearby at Norbury Park, were close friends. Their eldest son, William, was also

connexions were extensive, and he devoted a great portion of his time to what are termed bread-and-butter parties. This requires explanation. Bread-and-butter parties are those to which performers of talent are invited to dinner, or to a supper, where a little music is given in a friendly way in the evening. These parties gave birth to benefit concerts; for as the professors so invited could not satisfy their own butchers and bakers by such engagements, they hit on the expedient of taking annual benefits, to afford their exalted friends an opportunity of returning the favour by taking tickets.'
[6]   New York Public Library, Berg Collection, Susanna E. B. Phillips, holograph diary, 22 August 1788.

studying painting, and two other children, Augusta and Frederick ('Feddy'), are mentioned. The description of Scheener's arrival on the morning of 23 August, his reception and the eager discussion of plans for music-making is vivid. Susan's delight at the prospect of a musical feast was marred only by her terror at the thought of being asked to participate:

23 August 1788

Saturday morn^g as soon as breakfast was over I went into the garden to gather some flowers – from the furthest end of it I heard our bell ring – & as it was easily concluded it c^d only be a butcher, or some such person – I went on therefore composedly about my occupation but to my great surprise heard Fanny's voice calling to me in a few minutes – *'Cousin Edward is come Mamma & Mr Scheener'* – I hastened to join her, & hear the news confirmed, & as I approached the house saw the two welcome persons she had announced – I hastened towards them – & found Phillips & Norbury busy in receiving them – the latter on hearing Mr Scheener's name went up to him & said – *'but where is Mr Pleyel*[?]' – having observed I suppose that those two names were often named together – It amused him very much – They had not breakfasted, having set out in the Horsham Coach at seven in the morning – We therefore conducted them upstairs, whilst breakfast was preparing for them in the parlour – all was instantly in commotion, for I had not an idea of seeing them so early – nor indeed till eve^g when the Dorking Stage arrives, but if I was surprised I was much more pleased – *delighted* I may say to gain the whole of this day, as I found Mr Scheener w^d be obliged to leave us the following Tuesday – My Fanny has seen him, & I remember liked his appearance – & during this visit he justified the opinion we had thence formed of him – I think him a Gentlemanlike, liberal minded man, with a great sensibility of worth in others, & diffidence of his own ability – our dear Edward, whom we must always receive with joy, was particularly in spirits in accomp^g this great musical favourite of his & of ours – We had a very pleasant second breakfast, after wch Phillips introduced the two Gentlemen into his workshop, where Scheener was invited to bring some fiddles to repair – & whilst we were there, the welcome intelligence reached us that two Instruments were arrived by the Stage – Mr Scheener's violin, & Edward's Tenor – with some baggage & music – I heard wth very great joy that Mr Burney w^d come in the eve^g – had our poor Esther been able our musical party w^d have been *compleat* – The Gent^n returned to the workshop, & I was called to dear Mr Lock, who came to see after my cold, wch was gone – & who was much pleased to hear of Edward's arrival & curious to hear Scheener, wth whose name & music he had before been acquainted by Phillips & me – I readily undertook that he should – & promised we w^d go the next eve^g to Norbury, when Mr B. w^d be with us, wch on *every* occasion was now so desirable – Phillips came in & bro^t Edward wth him – Mr Scheener went to dress, & I was sorry not to be able to introduce him to Mr Lock, who soon after took his leave – Scheener then came to us, & enchanted by *trying* the different instruments – playing *little extempore touches* wth such delicacy & sweetness, that hearing such exquisite sounds so seldom as I do, I was *hors de moi* – *such* sounds are indeed rarely to be heard anywhere – for Scheener has a delicacy – a feeling – a *soul* in his playing, such as I think I have scarce ever met wth in more than 3 or 4 performers –

Pacchierotti & Fischer I rank in that number. Edward now retired to dress, & Mr Scheener pressed *me* to play! Oh dio! – How do you think I enjoyed this idea! – but unfortunately Phillips was in the room – and I was actually *compelled* to do it – & – all things considered got thro' one of Pleyell's new Sonatas, to wch there is a delightful accomp^t for the violin, better than – usual – I mean to any company – had Edward been there I had been undone – or indeed any *mere* listener – even Phillips did me no good – but Mr Scheener was as encouraging as possible, & paid me a great many flattering compliments on my *accuracy* in *time* & *expression* etc – He did all he c^d to prevent my regretting this terrifying performance & s^d the same kind of things to Edward at his return into the room, but I slip'd off, unwilling to risk my little credit by a second attempt – I kept the children with me till dinner, wch passed very pleasantly – after it I went wth them in the garden, & we were joined by the Gent^n who drove alternately Nordia & Fanny in their chaise – Scheener admired them most exceedingly – & s^d Fanny was *si bien elevé* – & had rec^d him so prettily on their arrival, when I was away, avec un maintien si doux – et une reverence si gracieuse that he was quite charmed with her – Nordia was out of his little wits wth rapture at the return of his dear cousin *Zezard*, as he thinks fit *jestingly* to call him since he has learn'd his letters – He was *the spirit of the party* – but ran up wth me on hearing coffee announced having obtained a promise of pouring it out – wch as we have it in a little *urn* with a spout, he can do perfectly well – at the same moment wth the coffee our dear Mr Lock came, accompanied by his sweet Mrs Lock – purposely I believe to invite Scheener in the most polite & elegant manner for the next day, as well as to claim *Edward's promise* – He behaved quite perfectly – feeling it [a portrait] *must* be done, he resisted making any attempt to elude our expectations, or disappoint our hopes – He was most *gracieusement* & sweetly rec^d by our dearest Mrs Lock – She (& yet more Mr Lock) was exceedingly amused by Nordia's employment – who full of bustle & eagerness, required almost all my attention, as he was pouring out the coffee – '*You shall have a dish*', s^d he, to Mrs Lock wth a little nod of his head – & seizing a lump of sugar wth his little fat fingers, he was going to pop it in, but I was just quick enough to stop him – 'Oh *do* let him alone', cried Mr Lock laughing – Nordia understood immediately that he ought to have used the tongs, & seizing the same lump of sugar from the tea board whilst he held the tea tongs in the other hand, he very dextrously put it into them, & I had a second struggle to save the dish of coffee from receiving it – wth some reluctance he relinquished it being allowed to choose another lump from the sugar dish – & having made a cup for Cousin Edward & Mr Scheener, I carried him off to his maid – finding he engrossed my attention something *too* much – 'Il faut avoir bien de la force pour lui rien refuser', s^d Scheener – 'et surtout lorsque c'est a sa Maman qu'il s'adresse – Il a un petit air si fin – et si *caressant* a la fois' – Our sweet friends stayed but a little – it was agreed that we sh^d shew Mr Scheener Norbury the next eve^g & spend it there. He was very much struck by our guests – even *particularly* with Mr Lock, who had conversed wth him about Geneva, from wch place Mr Scheener comes – We were speaking of him together when Mr Burney arrived – much to the satisfaction of the whole party but particularly to *mine* – who had, added to other motives, one *selfish* [one] for too rejoicing at his arrival – no music c^d otherwise have been obtained that *I* sh^d perfectly have enjoyed – If our poor Esther had been of the party! – It w^d then have been very compleat – Mr B. was in excellent spirits & we had a most charming eve^g – tried over 5 new quartettos of Pleyell wch are delicious, & wch Mr Scheener played most *exquisitely* – I was obliged to play the violoncello part as well as I was able on the Piano Forte – but even in spite of that disadvantage, it was a charming performance, & I listened to it with unspeakable delight. At night we all parted apparently pleased with our day – What a treat this was! – My Fanny will I am sure rejoice that I had it.[7]

Complimenting the behaviour and accomplishments of any children present was something no professional musician could ignore. Scheener showed himself fluent in the necessary pleasantries. The next, and more delicate, stage was to encourage his reluctant hostess to perform herself. A certain measure of insistence on the part of a professional showed good breeding, as it would be seen as an acknowledgement of the accomplishment of the amateur, but cajoling could not be pushed too far. As an amateur who prided herself on her discriminating taste but was well aware of her technical limitations, Susan knew that during the course of the weekend she would face the exquisitely painful dilemma of deciding how much she could risk playing. At first all went well:

The next morn^g Sunday Augt 24th was wet, & chiefly spent within doors – our Church is now repairing – Mr Scheener Mr B. & Edward tried over some fine trios by Schwindl & Pleyell before dinner. After it he was so good as to take a great deal of trouble to persuade *me* to play another lesson wth him – & pressed it so much & so goodhumour'dly that had not Mr B. come in to my relief I know not how I sh^d have escaped – He however spared me any conflict very comfortably by sitting down to play the lesson Schuner was tempting me to attempt himself – & the latter then gave up pressing me further, perceiving what perfectly lost time it w^d be – The carriage came for us at 6 – & we went in it wth the Instruments & Music – Scheener pleased me very much by the pleasure *He* testified in seeing Norbury Park, & by his astonishment & delight when he entered the drawing room, wch was kept from breaking out only by his modesty – We were most gladly welcomed, & Mrs Lock told me Augusta had vented her raptures in loud screams for near half an hour, upon hearing the pleasures in store for her that evening. Mr Lock was very attentive to our *Genevois*, & finding him fond of drawings & paintings shewed him a great many – After Tea, & a little tuning by Mr Burney, he began [our?] *concert* by a spirited overture on the Piano Forte – this over – Scheener *waked to rapture all the trembling strings* – we had the delicious quartettos, in wch I accomp^d wth much panic – tho' the pleasure of listening to such sounds soon overcame it – It was truely felt & enjoyed too by the party, & Scheener played *con amore* – a more perfect performance I never heard – nor *so* exquisite a one on that Instrument – We had some *organ music* between, & Mr B. played some of Pleyell's Sonatas accomp^d by Mr Scheener.

Susan's anxieties now rapidly increased. The imminence of Charles Burney's departure placed her in the unenviable position of being the only remaining keyboard player. With her friend pressing her for further music-making, she could foresee only too clearly what was likely to happen:

My dearest Mrs Lock finding he was to stay wth us till Tuesday, grew very anxious to have another meeting – but as Mr B. was going next day, I confess I wished to have spent it at home – feeling that after having had him he w^d be so missed that all w^d be *manquée*, & that I sh^d be called upon, & almost compelled to undertake a thousand things I sh^d be unable to execute – so that I c^d not help dreading the thoughts of it – however her urgency prevailed – & upon mentioning it to Mr Lock, he beg'd we w^d let them have the morning of the next day, as Mr B. c^d stay till after dinner – promising he sh^d have it at any hour he pleased – It was agreed to be at 3 o'clock precisely – We were then petitioned to give the *whole* morn^g by coming to Breakfast, & as Mr Scheener had hurt his ankle, the carriage was to be sent for us at half past nine – It was privately agreed upon between Mrs Lock & me that in the eve^g when Mr B. was gone Edward should begin his picture – & at night she promised we sh^d go home, or stay without music, unless Mr Scheener & Edward c^d play any duets together – We all came away well pleased – Scheener *thanked* me repeatedly for having procured him the honour of an introduction to M^r & Mrs Lock – & as we drove from the door exclaimed as Pacchierotti w^d have done had he spent an eve^g in such society 'What a *Charming* Family!' – He shewed a great deal of observation in his remarks on the bonté & douceur that appeared in the countenance & manner of Mrs Lock – the beauty of the children, & the *finesse* there was in all that Mr Lock spoke – his perfect *amabilité* – wit – & *refined politeness* – I was doubly pleased with him upon observing he c^d so well discriminate, & feel wth so much sensibility the excellencies of this incomparable family – & I admired very truely his own unassuming modesty, wch made him regard his introduction there as a favour to himself, instead of considering the exquisite pleasure he had bestowed on them as an obligation we all owed to him – The sweet music I had heard, & the idea of that I *sh^d* hear, & in such society too, the next day, absolutely deprived me of sleep – I arose very early Monday 25th Aug^t & at the appointed hour Mr Scheener being ready he accomp^d me in the carriage up the hill – Phillips walked wth Mr B. & Edward – It was a beautiful morning, & they had all the pleasure of seeing Norbury in very great perfection – My sweet Mrs Lock rec^d us wth delight – & we had – a *Norbury Breakfast* – My Fanny knows what that is – the dear girls breakfast & dine wth them now constantly – & Feddy too, on this occasion, by his own particular desire – & he behaved admirably –

We had scarcely entered the Drawing Room after breakfast when news was bro^t of the arrival of a party who wanted to see it – So we all went into the Library, & the time was well spent in examining some of Mr William's drawings, tho' it was a little *grudged* by Mrs Lock, & Augusta, who is really extremely fond of music – & when this *visitation* was over we returned into the Drawing Room, & there *made music*, w^th *great success*, & *incessantly*, till dinner was announced at 3 o'clock – it was the first bad sound that had reached our ears that day – our dear Mrs Lock had determined to make Scheener *amends* (if he was an Epicure) for his trouble, for we found a table spread largely with delicacies – fish, fowls, *venison* & *Majaroni, Ices*, etc etc but he did not disappoint the expectations I had conceived of him, for he was nearly as temperate as the incomparable master of the house. He enjoyed however the dinner, tho' not simply the food – indeed it was very charming – We had all been highly gratified, & every one was in spirits – I was obliged to remind poor Mr Burney he must go after dinner for indeed I feared his being in the dark – & he left us and we parted from him not without regret, but wth many pleasant recollections

– My sister says she never heard him so animated in the praise of any place or people as he has been on this occasion – When he was gone, a walk was proposed to Mr Scheener – Mr Lock went on Jenny – Mr William & Phillips walked wth Mr Scheener – Edward was called by Mr Lock to be of the party – but we had agreed it w^d be best for him to attempt beginning Feddy [his portrait] – I therefore cried out *He* must not go.

It seems fairly clear from the above description that Scheener's recompense for his efforts was pleasant company, extravagant compliments, good food, country air, elegant surroundings: everything but a fee.

When tea was over, Susan, to her great chagrin, was effectively ambushed by Mrs Lock. Despite their previous agreement that Susan should not be required to perform beyond her ability, there was a general move for more music:

We had tea & then a little general conversation but it soon flagged – there were violins, & music, & every body longing to hear Scheener – & all looked towards *me* as being the only person who c^d give him a *Base* – but – think how pleasant – terrified as I must at any rate have been to play wth Scheener alone, there was no music wth any accomp^{ts} that I c^d play except two of Pleyell's new lessons, very difficult, & wch I had not above half learne'd, & wch Mr Burney had played the ev^g before & again that morn^g – However *pour abreger* I was obliged to go thro', frightened to death, both lessons – & then accomp^d as well as I c^d a new trio of Haydn's – after wch I was half *compelled* to begin a lesson of Kozeluch's I had not seen these two years, & of wch I c^d not get thro' the first page – & after all – suffering very unpleasant sensations, & forcing myself to attempt what I knew I c^d not execute, it ended as I had foreseen, in general disappointment – chiefly on the part of my dear Mrs Lock – who tho' she w^d attempt nothing herself, seemed to think *I* ought to undertake everything – believing me capable of what I am not perhaps – but indeed fear disabled me compleatly – & rendered things difficult to me wch alone w^d have had nothing to alarm me – Had she permitted me as I wished to have gone home after tea wth our party, & wch as we had been there ever since tea in the morning, & Scheener was to set out early next day, w^d not have been unpleasant to *him*, instead of remaining where we were till midnight, the sweet recollections of the morning w^d not have been spoiled, & we sh^d have concluded the day as well as it had been begun – but where anything is so feelingly enjoyed it is difficult to stop whilst there is the least hope of continuance – I c^d not but be very sorry – & vexed – & share the disappointment which I *seemed* to have occasioned – tho' only because more had been expected from me than I *could* execute.

Scheener left Norbury Park with the usual expressions of regret, claiming his indebtedness to Susan for his introduction to the Locks in terms so fulsome that she felt 'quite ashamed' as she felt 'the obligation was on *our* side'. He agreed to wait for the second coach, which was due around noon the following day. In the morning, whilst waiting, he tried over 'a set of Kozeluch' with Susan, which she thought she played 'pretty ill', despite receiving 'a number of goodnatured & encouraging speeches from Mr Scheener – too flattering for me to repeat'. When the stagecoach passed through Mickleham it was full, and Scheener was obliged to stay on an extra day. The slightest hint of regret or vexation would have been out of the question. With the renewed possibility of music-making at Norbury Park, Susan was determined to get some ground rules for her participation agreed with Mrs Lock:

I left off at the 26th Augt when the stage having disappointed Mr Scheener, in the most polite & flattering manner *il prit son partie*, & determined to enjoy & *shew* that he enjoyed all the pleasure the country & satisfaction his admirers & friends could give him – Edward had been expected at Norbury I knew to proceed in his picture, & I had promised to accompany him – but as we c^d not leave Scheener, & I was likewise certain he w^d be a very welcome guest I proposed to him to be of the party – He readily agreed, & we set out, Captⁿ Phillips promising to follow. When we arrived at the end of our pleasant walk, Scheener from motives of delicacy wished to have strolled in the park during our visit, to wch however you may be sure I did not agree – Mrs Lock was very much surprised but yet more delighted to see us, & hearing we sh^d yet have another day of Mr Scheener's company, in a manner not to be resisted pressed us to let it be passed where we were, & that the children might be brought to join us – Edward ran off to prepare his palette & colours for Feddy – I sat down to write to Phillips for the children etc, & Scheener pressed me exceedingly to suffer him to go down the Hill for them – but whilst this was arguing, Phillips arrived – who immediately said *He* would be the messenger, & then Mr Scheener was not to be diverted from accompanying him – Mrs Lock & I being then alone we talked over the disappointment of the preceding evening, & made a *virtuous* resolution that all sh^d be done we c^d any of us to prevent the present from turning out in the same manner – I gained from her a promise not to be pressed to undertake anything *absolutely* out of my power to perform, assuring her at the same time that whatever I c^d undertake when we were alone, I w^d make an effort to do if wished for on the present occasion – but I told her she must assist on her part, & *sing* – to wch she gave a *melancholly* assent – but with far greater alacrity declared Augusta sh^d play a lesson – this was I thought like the French ladies in lent – '*Faisons jeuner nos valets*' – but it w^d have been too sawcy to have said so – I offered to hear Augusta play a lesson wch has an accomp^t to know what chance there w^d be of its going off tolerably – however we were soon all to powder & prepare for dinner, & there was no opportunity for this till evening.

During the afternoon, a walk was proposed. Susan remained behind, but her attempts to prepare for the evening's 'concert' were thwarted by the inability of Augusta, her 'pupil', to respond to last-minute attempts to rectify mistakes thoroughly learned:

I had then an opportunity of hearing Augusta in a lesson of Pleyell's which, if *any*, she wished to play – I was sorry to find she made innumerable & very bad errors in the time, stop'd her, & tried to remedy all those that were likely to affect the accomp^t – but there was no time for her to practice after my lesson, & she had so *grounded herself* in her mistakes, that I began to wish her playing had not been proposed, & to be sorry our dear Mrs Lock w^d venture it – I felt *myself* dreadfully in want of practice, & w^d have given *something*, for an hour or two by myself, but we c^d not even try a duet, as the tea appeared before Augusta's lesson was done, & in a few minutes the walkers arrived, much delighted wth their ramble. We had tea, & after it & Feddy's hearing many tunes from Edward before he w^d go to bed, Mr Scheener at the first word & with the most obliging readiness took his violin – He looked over the music wch had been brought, & fixed upon Schwindl's Trios to begin, & I was seated at the organ to play basso – wch as the accomp^t is easy, & I was determined to command myself as well as I c^d I got thro' pretty well, wth much encouragement from my *Friend* Mr Scheener – We played two of these – wch comparing them to Pleyell's appeared flat tho' they are very pretty – Edward had then the wickedness to propose a *Kozeluch* – I believe only to escape from the violin himself – I was bound to refuse nothing I c^d undertake – and so played one – but by Mr Scheener's desire on the organ instead of the Piano Forte wch was very much against me, the touch being so much heavier – He however insisted it went very well – We had then an adagio of Pleyell's in wch Edward joined – & after it Mrs Lock's song was beg'd for – She did all she c^d but was unable, tho' wth every encouragement on the part of Scheener to get entirely thro' it – wch she however promised to do *after supper* – Then Augusta's lesson was mentioned – & wth a little reluctance the poor thing sat down to play it – I got out of sight & at a little distance – I was indeed sorry & ashamed at this part of the eve^gs performance – M^r & Mrs Lock sat by Augusta to encourage her, & Scheener got on wth her wonderfully well – supporting her where feeble, slackening his pace, & quickening it again just as she did, & managing so adroitly that Edward who was employed in looking over drawings wth Mr William, & who was unacquainted wth the lesson previously thought as he afterwards told me it went very tolerably – to my great surprise my dear Mrs Lock seemed to think so too – because there had been no *absolute stop* – thanks to the *accompaniment* & when Scheener made some little compliment, she told him Augusta was *my scholar* – Scheener then turned his eyes on me wth a look so comically expressive, that I was convinced *he* at least felt that I was aware of all in which my pupil had failed – & I had such a consciousness of [deleted] being so upon me that I c^d not meet his eyes – he asked me if I played these lessons, refusing to believe I did not – but I turned away to speak to somebody else, feeling unwilling to enter into any conversation about it – He perhaps saw this – for he afterwards spoke of every other part of the eve^gs performance except this.

The stiffest test of the social skills of a society violinist came when asked to accompany the dire efforts of a well-meaning lady amateur (the gentlemen dilettante was supposed to be awful) or, worse still, of a child in the presence of its parents. Scheener passed the test with consummate ease, adapting his part to avoid what would have been the ultimate shame for a young woman, the complete breakdown of the piece, but at the same time indicating to the musically acute Susan his awareness of what was really happening. The reluctant Mrs Lock could now find no further excuse but took refuge in a duet rather than a solo:

Mrs Lock was beg'd to resume her song – but resisting Mrs Lock beg'd to have a *Duet* – & so poor I came *sur le tapis* again – We chose as the easiest as well as I think one of the prettiest Aprile's *'T'intendo, si mio cor'* wch I believe you have heard – I did all I c^d to sing steadily – but when one is frightened, the voice will either tremble, or become *hard* I think – however Mr Scheener expressed himself as much pleased as if it had been a very charming performance, & beg'd to have it repeated – Mrs Lock without reluctance complied – I c^d not refuse being only *second*, tho' I think it must have been a great bore to him –

We then prevailed on him to play two *Themes* wth variations of Pleyell's, missing the Tenor Part – & play them he did so deliciously that the recollection will always be sweet to me – Supper had then been waiting half an hour, & we were oblig'd to go to it – It passed very pleasantly.

Upon taking his final leave, there were the usual expressions of mutual courtesy. Susan noted Scheener's appreciation of the gracious style of living that he had enjoyed over the past few days and recorded his dissatisfaction with his profession and the amount of effort it required to maintain a high standard:

At parting Scheener rec^d a general & most flattering invitation from Mr Lock to his house at any time when he might wish for a little country air – & every mark of polite & pleased attention from Mr Lock, & even from Mr William, who was extremely *taken with him* – It was not thrown away, for Scheener was quite touched by it – & told me so often how *infiniment obligé* he was to me for having introduced him in to that family, that I was almost ashamed of hearing him. He often reminded me of Pacchierotti by the enjoyment he seems to have of refined society – & by his disatisfaction wth his profession, from its requiring so much time & labour, that it renders a man incapable of acquiring anything else – 'Il faut une application continuelle pour parvenir à etre un degré plus haut qu'un *Ripieno*.'

Susan Burney's eloquent account of Scheener's stay at Mickleham illustrates the distinctive features of the country visit. By its very nature such a visit was a special occasion. Away from London, ardent amateur music-lovers could face lengthy periods of musical famine, all the more insupportable after the intense delights of the season. A visit from a top-quality professional was thus highly prized. Free from the pressures of life in the capital city, the conduct of music-making was relaxed, with informal sessions interspersed with country pursuits such as walking or fishing. More than was usually the case in London society, music-making took place with family members of all ages present, and dealing tactfully with children and young people was an important skill for the musician. Another was flexibility: the ability and experience to choose repertoire suited to limited talents and incomplete forces. In all respects, Scheener's performance during his visit was exemplary, both socially and musically, and by the end he was being treated as a family friend. His reward was to establish for himself a regular position in the musical soirées organized by the Burneys in London during the season. Although he was not really in the running for a major London appointment, regular private engagements with so high-profile a musical family would greatly enhance his reputation and doubtless bring numerous useful contacts.

3

The London Season

Although social etiquette and musical taste were the same in London as in the country, the organizational dynamic of a private musical party was very different in the urban context. Pressure of time was of much greater significance. For top professional musicians, full diaries and potentially conflicting engagements imposed new challenges to tact and diplomacy. But the availability of a pool of players looking for work meant that there was rarely any need for a continuo part to be missing, or for a quartet to lack its inner parts. A 'society' violinist charged with the organization of a private concert could much more easily obtain the required musical resources, but there would now be the possibility of comparison. A sub-standard performance would be much more noticeable in this context, and it was necessary to contend with male amateurs, often more prominent than in the rural context, who could be relied on to provide execrable playing. In the light of Susan Burney's account of Scheener's deft handling of his country visit, it will be interesting to see him in action in London during the season, where he was a regular guest at the musical soirées organized by Esther and Charles at their Titchfield Street home.

Esther was as enthused by Scheener's playing as Susan, and he soon became in effect 'violinist in residence' at Titchfield Street. During her next visit to London, Susan renewed her acquaintance with him:

28 September 1788

Just before tea Mr Scheener called – expecting to see us, as he had heard from Edward we sh^d be there – I was really glad to see him, & he seemed gayer than I ever saw him, & elated at seeing us – I hope he will give us another little visit at Mickleham before Xmas – I made tea for the party – our dear Esther had then dropped to sleep & as violins etc were prepared immediately after tea, I continued in the parlour, whence the sound did not reach to my sister's room. But tho' I heard 3 sweet Quartettos, I c^d but half enjoy them – anxious lest Esther sh^d be awakened & in pain, & at the end of the 3^d Quartetto the carriage came for us – I went up stairs & found my sister better, & very sweetly pleasing herself wth the thoughts of our being entertained below – I left her very reluctantly, & below stairs when I went in to say goodnight found Scheener just going to begin Lolli's solos, accomp^d by Mr B. on the violoncello, wch he had played in the Quartettos – I heard afterwards he went thro' them all exquisitely – but I c^d not stay for a note – Fanny was wth me, & the carriage waiting – I was very glad to have met wth him, & to find he still remembered wth pleasure his visit to us, to w^{ch} & to the Norbury family he was full of *allusions* in every thing he said – Mr Christian La Trobe was there, & attempted playing the tenor parts in the quartetts, in wch however he was frequently obliged to become a mute, not being a very good player on that Instrument – on the Piano Forte he is really an exceedingly good performer, & surprised me at my Father's by his masterly manner of executing some of Echardts & Haydn's music – as we returned home, Fanny unexpectedly amazed me by her remarks on the concert, wch she & Sophy had sat on the same chair listening to like very good children – She told me she liked it very much – that Mr Scheener she thought played *best of all* – & Cousin Edward *next* best – 'but M^r La Trobe', s^d she, 'did not play at all Mamma – very seldom indeed – only before the rest began sometimes he played a little by himself – & then when they began he did not play, & sometimes seemed to be *making believe* – but I wonder Mamma that my Uncle Burney should like to play on such a *great* violin! – Quite a *Monster!* – He *could not get it up under his chin*, so he was *obliged to hold it between his knees'* – I leave you to guess if I laughed![1]

When Susan next visited London in April 1789, her relief at once again being able to hear good performances of repertoire of interest comes across in her descriptions. (It had been six months since she was last there.) Scheener was still acting as resident professional. The personal warmth of Susan's relationship with him (and now his wife too) is very evident:

26 April 1789

There was to be music in the evening, but my little ones went before any one arrived – I think there were no other Ladies except Miss Young & Sarah – And Mrs Scheener, who came early, & to whom I beg'd my sister to introduce me – I sate by her the whole evening – She is little more than twenty, tall – & uncommonly large & fat for her age – indeed perhaps for any age – her face is handsome, & its expression feminine & pleasing – her voice & manners very soft – altogether, tho large, she gives you an idea of nothing masculine – she seems at once gentle, & gay – I liked her very much, & we conversed a great deal together – indeed I *wished* to like her for the sake of her Husband – & I believe he has made, for *happiness*, a very good choice, tho' they will not be overburthened by the *mammon of unrighteousness* – I sincerely hope I judge rightly – I renewed my acquaintance wth him wth much pleasure & found him modest, well bred, & pleasing as ever – before the eve^g was over Phillips renewed his invitation to him for the summer *with his wife* – wch was very kindly received, & we may probably see them for a little time when the London season is over.[2]

There is no reason to doubt the sincerity of Susan's observations, but her motive in promoting this 'friendship' was her intense desire to attract the Scheeners down to her Surrey home for a musical visit during the summer months. The concert soon got under way:

The Music was very excellent, & the Concert delightful tho' without any singing – We had several charming Quartettos by Pleyel in wch Scheener played exquisitely, & was admirably seconded by Mr Burney, Edward, & *Crosdill* – who played a Solo better than I ever heard him. His tone & execution are perfect, – & his style in general good – *Manca l'anima* alone! a *little* word wch prevents me

[1]   New York Public Library, Berg Collection, Susanna E. B. Phillips, holograph diary, 28 September 1788.
[2]   British Library, Egerton MS 3692, f. 14.

from ever enjoying [deleted word] *delight* in hearing him, tho' I never fail to admire his powers.[3] M[r] Burney played admirably – a cappriccio – a Mickleham theme – that is to say a Theme composed here last Winter, & the prettiest thing I think he ever composed – & a Duet wth his dear Wife who played likewise a very fine lesson by Kozeluch, & who never played better – After the first Quartetto, wth which the evening began, Miss Frye acquitted herself exceedingly well in a difficult lesson of Pleyell's – She is one of M[r] Burney's best scholars – We had sweet Quartettos between almost every performance – after supper we set down M[r] and M[rs] Scheener, who seemed not less pleased than we were wth the evening. They promised to meet us for a quite *private* party the next Tuesday in Titchfield Street.

Two days later, Susan met the violinist's wife again and described her as 'much undressed' and looking 'very pretty'. Another engagement for Scheener was quick in coming, arranged through the good offices of Susan's husband, Captain Phillips.[4]

By the early 1780s, quartet-playing had become extremely fashionable, and the 'quartet party' had established itself as one of the most popular genres of the domestic musical soirée. This certainly suited the 'society' violinist who would act as leader, supervising the efforts of amateur musicians. The next private concert described in the journal-letter was a quartet party, but it was musically less satisfying. The viola and cello players from the King's Theatre orchestra (supposedly one of the best in London) were disappointing, and one of the amateur performers, an Irish friend of the Burneys, attracted scornful comment:

29 April 1789

W[th] M[r] Fitz., M[r] Francis, & My Captain, M[r] Scheener came up stairs – & M[r] Scola, & M[r] Gehot – And – *M[r] Edward Burney*, whose sight is never *very* unwelcome to me. They soon began wth a Quartetto of Pleyell's – a delicious one – but poor Scheener was so abominably ill accomp[d], except by Edward, that it was to *him* very provoking, & to me a great disappointment, having flattered myself wth a charming regale of music. It quite ruined the Quartettos – Scola[5] is

[3] For all his technical proficiency, Crosdill sometimes failed to move discerning listeners. McVeigh, *Concert Life*, 145, cites the comment of a reviewer who wrote of the cellist: 'he surprizes, but he does not elevate'. Twining concurred. On 22 October 1783 he had written to Burney: 'nothing seems less extraordinary than a Musician with every requisite *but* feeling. Crosdill, to me, has absolutely *none*; nor Cramer.' *The Letters of Charles Burney*, ed. Ribeiro, i, 399.

[4] 'I was very fortunate this week in meeting with Scheener who thro' Phillips means was engaged at M[rs] FitzGerald's the following eve[ning].' British Library, Egerton MS 3692, f. 16.

[5] Charles Scola joined the King's Theatre orchestra in 1760 and was still there as late as 1792. Philip H. Highfill Jr, Kalman A. Burnim and Edward A. Langhans, *A Biographical Dictionary of Actors, Actresses, Musicians, Dancers, Managers and Other Stage Personnel in London 1660–1800*, 16 vols. (Carbondale, 1973–93), xiii, 235. In 1778, he was pilloried in the *Queen of Quavers* satire as the idiot who ended up attempting to give evidence for both prosecution and defence: 'I am Mr. Pimperlimpimp, *cognomento* Scola', he pathetically remarks. On this satire, see Woodfield, *Opera and Drama*, 166–81.

deaf & almost *blind* & continually played false bases – & Gehot[6] to my great surprise expressed every thing ill, & made frequent mistakes, even in the *notes* – yet both these men are of the opera band. Scheener still played admirably – but not with his pathetic & exquisite expressions, wch he was too ill at ease, being perpetually mortified by the ill effect of every thing from such vile accompaniments, ever to attempt – I was very sorry for him – He however gained great credit by playing *at sight* some Music bro^t by Scola wch as he & Gehot knew it, they accomp^d decently – & Edward, tho' at sight as well as Scheener, played it very well – After this he accomp^d Mrs Fitz.[7] in a spirited lesson of Kozeluch, wch she played very tamely, & truly *stumpingly* – I was surprised at it, as I heard her in some Music of Eichner's at Boulogne[8] & tho^t her an uncommonly good Lady Player. I suppose she had caught the manner from somebody else in that, & that she had taught herself this lesson of Kozeluch's. Scheener won everybody's heart by his accompaniment.

I was afterwards I am very sorry to relate, persecuted into attempting a lesson – & wth my usual ill luck on such occasions was compelled to play one in wch I was wholly out of practice – there being no Sets of Pleyells, or Haydn or Schroeters that I knew – I played in consequence additionally ill, & sh^d have been very angry wth myself for having made the attempt had it been in my power to avoid it – Scheener however tried to comfort me by saying he had not been so well accomp^d all the eve' as in my slow movement & other flattering things. I came away wth Charlotte & Mr Francis before the Music was quite done.

During his visit to Mickleham, Scheener had been able to indicate to Susan his awareness of Augusta Lock's shortcomings, but he could not possibly do so in response to her own admission of poor performance. The only acceptable response was flattery. To those with little musical self-awareness, it could be offered without reserve, but Susan Burney was both a very perceptive musician and a sharp critic of anything sub-standard. This made no difference at all. The necessity of behaving with impeccable politeness towards a host easily outweighed any considerations of musical honesty. Embarrassed by her own shortcomings, Susan nevertheless allowed herself to take some comfort from the violinist's words of support.

Relations with Scheener had become so warm by the time of the next soirée that Susan seemed willing to rank the violinist only a little below Pacchierotti – an honour indeed from a Burney! But this was only

---

[6] Joseph Gehot was in London by 1780 and in 1783 was playing in the King's Theatre orchestra, where he was still engaged in 1792. Highfill, Burnim and Langhans, *A Biographical Dictionary*, vi, 132.

[7] Mary Fitzgerald was a friend of the Burney girls. In a letter dated 4 November 1788 to his daughter Charlotte, Charles Burney describes her as 'our old Friend & favourite ... she has an original spirit & Character that w^d strike fire out of a Norfolk Turnip or Dumplin.' Fanny Burney, *The Early Journals and Letters*, ed. Lars E. Troide, ii (Oxford, 1990), 211.

[8] Eichner was often played by Esther Burney, as Fanny recalls: 'She [Miss Guest] began with playing the third of Eichner, and I wish she had begun with something else, for I have so often heard our dear Etty in this, that I was quite spoiled for Miss Guest, or, I firmly believe, for anybody; because in Eichner, as in Bach of Berlin, Echard and Boccherini, Etty plays as if inspired, and in taste, expression, delicacy, and feeling, leaves nothing to wish.' *Diary and Letters of Madame D'Arblay*, ed. Barrett, i, 358.

after receiving yet another extravagant compliment from the ever-attentive violinist:

30 April 1789

The Scheeners had very kindly been invited, & Mr Burney was fortunately at home for the whole Evening. Scheener in a very flattering manner, reproached me for not having played more the eve^g before – & called it a public theft. He was in great spirits, extremely pleased at meeting this party, & they at the sight of him. The most perfect harmony subsisted during the whole evening. We had three of Pleyells most exquisite Quartettos – I think certainly as I had the honour of choosing them. Scheener *played as if he had been at Norbury!* M^r & Mrs Lock certainly inspire him! When there & upon *this* evening he played far more exquisitely than elsewhere, or upon any other I have ever heard him – tho' he is always sweet & charming – but when I have heard him in these very select parties I think he has exceeded in touching & exquisite expression every instrumental Performer I have *ever heard*, & *save Pacchierotti* I c^d almost add every vocal performer too. He seems indeed to possess, to borrow the words of my dear Father 'that superior power of expressing almost all that a human *voice* can produce, except the articulation of the words'. But this, tho said of Violin Players in general, I think I c^d yet only say of Scheener.[9]

I was chosen *Maestro*, & gave my orders – in consequence of which after a Quartetto Esther played a New & exquisite Sonata of Haydn's[10] in wch she was most admirably accompanied by Mr Scheener – & after another Quartetto, Mr B. was accomp^d by him in a brilliant & delightful lesson of Pleyell's – Then we had a Trio of Viotti's[11] – Then a new Harpsichord Duet, & after infinite persuasion Mrs Lock, unaccompanied, sung two Airs, & our concert concluded by a 3^d delicious Quartetto ... It was one of the sweetest Musical evenings I ever spent.

Susan Burney's appointment as 'maestro' for the evening is significant. In domestic concerts, women could, if they so desired, exert a strong influence on repertoire and thereby ensure a socially acceptable balance between 'male' genres (such as the string quartet) and 'female' genres (such as the accompanied sonata).[12]

In establishing a position as the Burneys' favoured chamber violinist, Scheener was setting standards of social behaviour and appropriate domestic musicianship that any rival would have to match. With his public career apparently in serious decline, Salomon was shortly to try to make use of his continuing domestic connection with the Burney family in an attempt to win an important public position. He would not only have to outshine Scheener as a musician, he would also have to match his social performance.

[9] Burney, *A General History*, ed. Mercer, ii, 1021, refers more coolly to the 'accuracy and expression' of Scheener's playing.
[10] If this performance (on 30 April) was of one of the three sonatas Hob. XV/11–13, published in England by Longman & Broderip as *Three Sonatas for the Piano-Forte or Harpsichord, with Accompaniments for a Violin and Violoncello* (London, [1789]), then Esther had somehow got hold of an advance copy. Artaria & Co. announced publication of the work on 1 July in Vienna, while Longman & Broderip entered the works at Stationer's Hall on 22 June.
[11] Viotti's trios op. 2 were published in Paris as *Six trios à deux violons et basse*, c.1785.
[12] See Woodfield, *Music of the Raj*, 113–16.

4

A Career in Decline

In the late 1780s Salomon began to experience increasing difficulty in maintaining a position as a public leader, even as second choice to Cramer. In December 1787, he was advertised as leader of the forthcoming Mara Concerts,[1] but, despite the fact that he had been in partnership with the singer for the past four seasons, it was Raimondi who eventually led the series.[2] This left him for the first time in several years without a London subscription series to lead. He was thus not directly involved in the machinations that followed the celebrated 'quarrel' between Haydn and the Professional Concert. The details of this dispute, caused by the fact that Longman & Broderip, through their connections with Artaria, were able to publish Haydn's 'Paris' symphonies before the Professional Concert could present them as the star 'new' items of their 1788 season, are well known and need not be repeated here. What is of relevance, though, is the idea that the newspaper war of words which erupted a suspiciously long time after the actual event could have been black propaganda on behalf of the rival concert organization at the Pantheon, aimed at stirring up further trouble for Cramer with Haydn. As potential leader of a Pantheon series with Haydn, Salomon, if not a participant, was certainly an interested party. A hint of the continuing tension between the managements at Hanover Square and the Pantheon is seen in a brief spat that flared up (during the period of the quarrel) over the apparent refusal of the Pantheon to release Mara to substitute for Mrs Billington at Hanover Square during a period of illness. One newspaper deplored the fact that the entertainment of the public was being sacrificed 'to the private enmity between the *illustrious sons* of the *string* and *bow*'.[3] The allusion is veiled but clear.

A few days after this report, the attack on the Professional Concert began in earnest. The well-known paragraph entitled 'HAYDN'S DEFENCE' included as its fourth point:

The public have been repeatedly deluded by Newspaper paragraphs, into a belief that Mr. Haydn was engaged by the Committee to visit London, and

---

[1] 'Madame Mara again attempts a subscription concert at Willis's Rooms, in which she is to be aided by all the interest of the *corps diplomatique* – Salomon to be the leader.' *Gazetteer*, 1 December 1787. See McVeigh, 'The Professional Concert', 70.

[2] Ignazio Raimondi came to London in 1780. His popularity in the later 1780s owed a great deal to the phenomenal success of his 'Bataglia'. Highfill, Burnim and Langhans, *A Biographical Dictionary*, xii, 250.

[3] *Morning Post*, 25 March 1788.

assist at a certain Concert; the whole of which was fabricated to answer sinister purposes, and to impose on the credulity of a generous Nation.[4]

The claim that the Professional Concert had persistently misled the public into thinking that a visit from Haydn was imminent introduces an element completely foreign to the original dispute about the symphonies. So far as is known, there were no such press announcements before the start of the 1788 season, but they had been a regular feature in previous years. A second communication, also entitled 'HAYDN'S DEFENCE', attempted to answer many of the points raised in the vigorous debate stimulated by the original 'card'.[5] It ends with a veiled threat:

There is some reason to hope that Mr. Haydn will visit London, and compose for another Concert, when, without doubt, he will fully defend himself, support the character of an honourable man, as well as the greatest composer in music.

This reference to 'another concert' certainly suggests that the attack on the Professional Concert was the work of supporters of the Pantheon.

Salomon's personal role (if any) in all of this is unclear. Although not employed as leader for the 1788 series, he had a strong association with the Pantheon and firm hopes of leading another series there with Haydn as composer. An invitation from the Professional Concert to appear as a soloist (he had made single appearances in 1785 and 1786, but none in 1787) could be viewed as a gesture of reconciliation, but an amazing review of the performance suggests another motive:

SALOMON was never more admirable than in his concerto last night, but unfortunately just as he commenced it, a most formidable scent arose, to which Falstaff's 'compound of villanous smells' was absolute fragrence, and resisting all the perfumes that endeavoured to subdue it, cruelly persisted till his performance ended.[6]

Unruly behaviour – booing, hissing, organized claques and even the occasional riot – was commonplace in the heated atmosphere of the King's Theatre, but was very rare indeed in the decorous atmosphere of Hanover Square. While one should not rule out the law which says that if anything can go wrong it will at the most unfortunate moment and in the most embarrassing manner, this seems much too much of a coincidence. A stink bomb perhaps gave vent to the anger felt by some elements of the Professional Concert at the activities of this known associate of the rival Pantheon.

Salomon's desire to win a top London leadership fared no better in 1789. Rumours of a series promoted by Mara (which Salomon would

4   *The World*, 29 March 1788.
5   *Ibid.*, 12 April 1788.
6   *Morning Post*, 29 April 1788.

have been a strong contender to lead) came to nothing.[7] Looking at the decade as a whole, the number of times that Salomon's name is mentioned in London concert advertisements in Simon McVeigh's database illustrates a clear trend (see Figure 1). The fall on this chart, especially sharp in 1788 and 1789, represents Salomon's generally diminishing prospects as a 'public' leader. If a similar chart were drawn for Cramer, it would show no such decline.

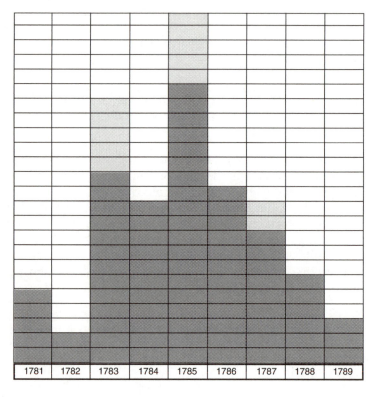

KEY

�(dark shading) advertised concerts excluding those which merely notify a replacement for Salomon

▢ additional unadvertised concerts in subscription series that Salomon is presumed to have led

Figure 1. London Concert Advertisements naming Salomon in the 1780s.

Statistics demonstrate clearly enough Salomon's declining public career; so too do one or two individual failures. His reputation in

---

[7] McVeigh, 'The Professional Concert', 74. There were also rumours of a visit by Mara to Dublin, where Salomon was engaged: 'It is said that all the efforts made to bring over Madam Mara to perform at the subscription concerts which were lately in agitation here have proved ineffectual.' *Freeman's Journal*, 2–5 May 1789.

London was not helped when his 1789 benefit concert flopped badly. Considering the large number of benefits that took place in eighteenth-century London, it is disappointing that there are so few eye-witness descriptions. Susan Burney's 1789 journal-letter provides useful accounts of two such performances she attended during her spring visit to London. The first was on behalf of Madame Gautherot, the woman violinist whose unusual choice of instrument was attracting much attention. The programme for her concert was advertised in the usual way:

Act I. Overture – Rosetti; Quartetto – Cramer, Blake, Shield & Smith; Song – Harrison; Concerto Horn – Pieltain; Song – Miss Cantelo; Concerto Violin – Gautherot.

Act II. Concertante Two Violins – Cramer & Gautherot; Sonata Pianoforte – Clementi; Song – Storace; Viotti Trio – Cramer, Gautherot & Smith; Duetto – Harrison & Cantelo; Symphony – Haydn.[8]

Gautherot, who had called to pay her respects to Burney, sold two tickets for her performance to Captain Phillips. Susan and Esther had hoped that Charlotte would accompany them, but Susan noted with amazement the response of her sister's Anglo-Indian husband Clement Francis, who said that '*he had not slaved so many years in India to pay half a guinea for any evening's entertainment – She might go if she pleased – but he neither w^d to that Consort or any other.*'[9] It was arranged that Susan would stay at Gautherot's benefit until about 10 o'clock, when a carriage would be sent to Hanover Square to take her on to Ranelagh, where her friends had set their hearts upon 'dear little Mrs Phillips' joining them. Susan expected to be so tired after this double engagement that she would 'scarce be able to see or stand'.[10] Gautherot's benefit is described thus:

1 May 1789

Cramer led, & played a Quartetto of Pleyell's very finely, but a little too much like a Machine – then Mr Harrison & Mrs Ambrose sung – both wth fine voices – yet tho' not vulgarly English, so cold & sleepy that it was difficult to keep ones eyes open, being likewise previously much tired. Mad^e Gautherot played a Violin Duet with Cramer – I was glad to see she was supposed to do herself

8   *Morning Post*, 28 April 1789.
9   British Library, Egerton MS 3692, f. 25^v. Clement Francis married Charlotte Burney in February 1786. He was a surgeon, who in India had acted as secretary to Warren Hastings. Joyce Hemlow, *The History of Fanny Burney* (Oxford, 1958), 193.
10   Tiredness increasingly affected her enjoyment of public performances. On 25 April 1789 she went to the King's Theatre to hear Marchesi: 'That eve^g James was taken wth a wish to hear Marchesi – Mrs Burney was too tired to go – but I accomp^d him willingly – yet I was too much fatigued to enjoy the opera much – but I was glad I went, as it proved the only opportunity I had whilst in town of so spending an eve^g. The opera was the Olimpiade, in which I had before heard Marchesi – but most of the songs were changed – I think for the worse – He sang very finely – for the rest I c^d scarce keep my eyes open so weary did I feel.' British Library, Egerton MS 3692, f. 13^v.

credit in it – but for my own part it seemed a great disadvantage to her – She executed all the passages – but it was wth evident Labour – Nothing was distinct – nothing clear – the powerful tone, the freedom – decision & most of all the perfect facility wth wch Cramer repeated every passage after her, disgraced all that she attempted, & betrayed the weakness & inferiority, wch tho' certainly it was no wonder to perceive, w^{d} have appeared far less glaring had she not subjected herself to so close & immediate a comparison. She has laboured infinitely there can be no doubt to attain such rapid execution, & so much precision, but in the most valuable points is I believe *very* inferiour to Sirmen indeed. It is true I heard Sirmen before I had heard any great Violin Players & now perhaps she w^{d} not seem so charming to me as she did in those early days – Yet still I am convinced she was far superiour in style & in feeling to Mad^{e} Gautherot. Miss Cantelo sang & I liked her better than I expected – She seems not *wholly* devoid of feeling, like most of our songstresses. In the 2nd Act Mad^{e} Gautherot executed a Trio of Viotti's – The same in wch the preceding eve^{g} I had heard Scheener. Poor woman – it w^{d} have been unfortunate for her if many in the room had had the same luck – however as it is Music rather brilliant than touching, she executed it exceedingly well. I forgot how the pieces followed, but I was oblig^{d} by the hour to leave the concert just as Storace was going to Sing wch I was really sorry to do.[11]

Overall, the programme seems to have been close to that advertised, with some minor changes in the order and one additional singer. Susan clearly felt that Gautherot's playing lacked the power and brilliance of the best male players.[12] Interest in the violin by women, both professional and amateur, was still confined to a few individuals willing to confront the almost universally accepted convention that the violin was an instrument fit only for male musicians.[13]

[11] British Library, Egerton MS 3692, f. 26.

[12] As Susan Burney realized, her views on Sirmen were perhaps coloured by the fact that she was young when she heard her. Susan was born in 1755 and would therefore have been 15 or 16 years old when Sirmen visited London in 1771 or 1772. Highfill, Burnim and Langhans, *A Biographical Dictionary*, xiv, 102–3. Although Cramer played at Gautherot's benefit, there were hints in the press of tension between the two. McVeigh, 'The Professional Concert', 18. On Gautherot see Highfill, Burnim and Langhans, *A Biographical Dictionary*, vi, 130.

[13] The previous year in Surrey, Susan had heard an accomplished amateur woman player, who caused quite a stir: 'Mrs Leaves is a very pleasing & [unclear] woman, & much admired for her *violin* playing – I was curious to hear, & sh^{d} have been much surprised at her excellence had I heard nothing about her previously – her execution is extremely neat & delicate, & she is an excellent musician – but the tone of her instrument is I think spoilt by the manner in which she holds it, (something like a Viol da Gamba) – she rests it on her knee, & her taste seems to me *at least* twenty years old – I will not therefore pretend to say her performance after my curiosity was gratified c^{d} ever give me much pleasure, tho' I admired her knowledge, precision, & facility very much – there was no other company than a M^{r} & Mrs Tillard of Leatherhead, rich good humoured, vulgar people – The overture was comic from the vile playing – Mrs Leaves & Mr Burney as 1st & 2nd Fiddle were indeed excellent – but Mr Leaves plays the Base very ill – Mr Eckersall the tenor much worse, & Mr Tillard was quite laughably wrong on the violoncello throughout the whole piece! – We had then the relief of a Sonata by Mr Burney – afterwards a Trio, an uncouth & not very pleasing composition of Mr Leaves's – then a song by Mrs Eckersall accomp^{d} on the Harp – her voice is so fine, & her figure so beautiful at the Instrument, that

Susan Burney's account of Salomon's benefit on 5 May 1789 reports in a matter-of-fact tone what appears to have been a serious failure. The Burneys had been given free tickets, and they were there as a party:

Act I. Overture – Haydn; Quartetto – Pleyel; Song – Ambrose; Concerto Violin – Salomon; Duetto – Miss Abrams; Concertante Piano, Violin & Violoncello – Clementi; Chorus 'On his Majesty's Happy Recovery' – Salomon.

Act II. Cantata – Federici.

Salomon ended the first half of the 1789 benefit with a highly topical piece, his chorus celebrating the recent recovery of George III. In her evocative description of the public illuminations arranged to mark the king's recovery, Papendiek recalls that Salomon travelled with her party to Kew 'in a glass coach', perhaps to witness the memorable moment when George met his whole family again.[14] The chorus was first given in public at the concert for The New Musical Fund on 13 April and was then repeated at its composer's benefit. Susan Burney was unimpressed with it. But it was his choice of a cantata for the second half of the concert that quite literally drove the audience out of the room:

5 May 1789

In the Eve^g I chapron'd Miss Young & I went to Salomon's benefit & met Esther – & Mr B. & Edward and Richard – & my dear Father. I think I saw few more of *my* acquaintances, tho numbers I know of Esther's. Salomon played a Quartetto of Pleyells in wch he was nearly as well accomp^d as Scheener had been at Mr Fitzgerald's [i.e. very badly] – but *He* did not satisfy me so well in his part as Scheener had done – Yet he is a most charming player – the Singers were Harrison & Mrs Ambrose – & the two Miss Abrams – who sung a Duet extremely well – I think we had nothing else in the first act but a Concerto by Salomon in wch he played finely, but I did not like the Music; & a *Chorus* upon the recovery of his Majesty – Our chorus singing is never exquisite – but in the *words* I believe all hearts tho' not all Voices joined.

The Second Act consisted of a Cantata the Music very good by Federici, tho' rather monotonous & lugubre, wch being sung only by Mr Harrison & Mrs Ambrose, was tedious & heavy beyond most things I have heard – before it was concluded, almost every body had been driven from the Room – I was sorry for poor Salomon – He spoke a few words to me at the end of the Concert, in

---

notwithstanding all deficiencies this was one of the most pleasing performances of the Evening – then a quartetto of Haydn's – & a Glee, the words Mr Eckersall's, the music Mr Leaves' – this was really a very pretty thing as was another the words from Beaumont & Fletcher in praise of *melancholly* – both these are engraved in different parts of Mr Eckersall's grounds – the singers were Mr Leaves, Mrs Leaves, & Mrs Eckersall – between these we had another lesson by Mr Burney, & they concluded wth a Quartetto of Haydn's.' New York Public Library, Berg Collection, Susanna E. B. Phillips, holograph diary, 20 June 1788. Remarkably, Susanna reports that that the following day the violinist gave birth unexpectedly to a son, much to the discomforture of Fanny, who was hoping to see 'the Lady that plays on the Violin'!
[14] Papendiek, *Court and Private Life*, ii, 68–70.

evident vexation & low spirits. I had met him a few days before at my Father's, where he had renewed his acquaintance wth me very pleasantly. He is going to Ireland & Phillips has given him letters there.[15]

Apart from the quality of Federici's music, one explanation for the vanishing audience may have been the length of the concert. Salomon had already been criticized for the excessive length of his benefit the previous year. The *Morning Post* of 13 March 1788 observed: 'If the entertainment had not been so good, the concert might have been deemed too long as it extended much beyond twelve o'clock.'[16]

Once his benefit of 5 May was over, Salomon had no pressing reason to stay in London, and he therefore took an engagement in Dublin. Working outside the capital city during the summer was a normal part of the annual professional calendar. Prestigious leaders were in demand at provincial festivals, Cambridge and Oxford in late June/early July, and Salisbury and Winchester in late September/early October. This type of seasonal engagement provided valuable employment for top London violinists in the lean summer months.[17] A profitable alternative to the English festivals had from time to time been provided by the annual season of summer concerts at the Rotunda in Dublin.[18] At the height of its popularity, this series consisted of 63 concerts over a period of 21 weeks from mid-May to mid-September. The fee of 100 guineas paid to the regular local leader Pinto was doubled whenever a major violinist was hired from London: Barthelemon (1771 and 1772); Cramer (1774); and Lamotte (1778). The 200 guineas paid to Cramer comfortably exceeded the £150 he received for leading at the King's Theatre in London. The timing of the Rotunda series made it a rewarding situation for a player engaged in London during the winter season, even though there was sometimes a small overlap to be negotiated.[19] By the mid-1780s, the Rotunda concerts were in very serious trouble. Dwindling audiences led to severe financial

[15] British Library, Egerton MS 3692, entry for Tuesday 5 May 1789.
[16] See also McVeigh, 'The Professional Concert', 4.
[17] An examination of engagements during the early 1780s makes it clear that Cramer and Salomon had the pick of the provincial leaderships, but it is also evident that Cramer was the first choice. The summer itinerary for a musician of his calibre could be very demanding, but it was also doubtless lucrative. In 1784 he played in Liverpool (14–17 September), Salisbury (22–24 September) and Winchester (29 September–1 October). See Douglas J. Reid and Brian Pritchard, 'Some Festival Programmes of the Eighteenth and Nineteenth Centuries: 1. Salisbury and Winchester; 2. Cambridge and Oxford; 3. Liverpool and Manchester', *Research Chronicle of the Royal Musical Association*, 5 (1965), 51–79; 6 (1966), 3–22; 7 (1967), 1–27. The itineraries followed by professional musicians during the summer months would make a rewarding study.
[18] Brian Boydell, *Rotunda Music in Eighteenth-Century Dublin* (Dublin, 1992).
[19] In the Rotunda minutes for 29 October 1778 (after Lamotte's departure) it was 'resolved that in future Agreements with foreign Performers, it shall be expressly stipulated, that a fortnight's Proportion of each Person's Salary shall be deducted for every Week he shall be absent after the Day fixed upon for opening the Rotunda for Summer Entertainments.' *Ibid.*, 113.

problems, which in turn led to a reduction in the length of the season. A succession of leaders from London – Scheener (1783); Barthelemon (1784); Raimondi (1785); Weichsell (1786, 1787 and 1788) – failed to halt the decline. When Salomon arrived in Dublin in May 1789, it was therefore to preside over a much-attenuated series which, as it turned out, was on the verge of complete collapse. Salomon certainly believed his engagement to be for three months, but in the event a mere 12 concerts (twice weekly on Wednesdays and Fridays) were scheduled to begin on 29 May. It is not even certain that all these took place. Having advertised for subscribers for several weeks, the organizers were then obliged to place an annoucement in *Freeman's Journal* of 26–28 May, implying that too few had so far come forward: 'The CONCERTS at the ROTUNDA, or PUBLIC ROOMS, which were advertised to begin on Friday the 29th instant, are obliged to be deferred to some future day,' of which public notice will be given.' The Rotunda Concerts were in irreversible decline, and the series did in fact cease two seasons later.

In addition to the Rotunda concerts, Salomon had also been hired to lead the oratorios put on by the Society of Musicians as part of the Commemoration of Handel. The first of these took place on Saturday 16 May at St Thomas's Church, and it was deemed to have been poorly attended. In an attempt to boost the audience, the *Dublin Journal* published a puff for the second performance, in which the abilities of the leader from London were singled out for praise: 'Exclusive of the general conduct of the Orchestra, one of the finest Concertos of Handel's composition has been chosen for the display of the distinguished abilities and execution of Mr. Salomon.'[20] The puff lays great emphasis on Salomon's ability as a leader, but in doing so implies that the first performance had needed firmer direction: 'the band ... has acquired additional steadiness and precision since the first day, under the training of so able a leader as Mr. Salomon'. *Freeman's Journal* further emphasized Salomon's strengths as a leader:

Mr Salomon, who led it [the first performance], possesses the best requisites of his profession, strength, yet delicacy of tone, and firmness of execution. His manner of leading had great merit, as it displayed a combining force, a concentrating power, that kept the band perfectly together and prevented the slightest deviation.[21]

As we have already seen, puffs were sometimes 'planted' for a specific purpose, to praise aspects of performance hitherto deemed to be weak. In view of the earlier reservations about Salomon as a Handel player, it is interesting to note that the *Dublin Journal* thought that his performance of Handel's 'eleventh grand concerto' was 'uncommonly elegant'. It was regretted that the 'wretched' second oboe had 'ruined

20   *Dublin Journal*, 19–21 May 1789.
21   *Freeman's Journal*, 19–21 May 1789. Cited by Ita Hogan, *Anglo-Irish Music* (Cork, 1966), 78.

everything in which the hautboys were concerned', and there had been one unfortunate absentee – Kotzwara, the principal double bass, who was doing who knows what! Nonetheless, the review ends with extravagant praise of Salomon's Handel playing: his execution of the concerto had been in that 'masterly style and expressive manner which could be expected only from those FEW masters who understand the genius of Handel, and amongst whom we rank Mr. Salomon'. His years in England had doubtless taught him much about the performance of Handel, but the tone of the piece again hints at something planted to counter an established perception. Salomon's Dublin benefit was on 23 June. He performed for the loyal Irish audience his chorus 'On His Majesty's Recovery', but the concert is more notable for the performance of a 'New Overture (Manuscript) – Mozart'.[22] Salomon made the best of his disappointment by looking for other opportunities. In *Walker's Hibernian Magazine* for June 1789, for example, it was reported that: 'Last Night, the Amateur Society gave a concert to an elegant and brilliant company of ladies of the first fashion, at which the celebrated Salomon, Sperati, and Mahoun assisted.' Nevertheless, Salomon's stay in Dublin was probably less lucrative than he had imagined it would be. He returned to London some time during the summer of 1789, probably soon after John Mahon's benefit on 14 July, at which he performed.

---

[22] Woodfield, 'John Bland', 233.

5

The Pantheon Leadership

Despite the embarrassment of the 'quarrel' with Haydn, it was becoming increasingly evident in 1788 that the Professional Concert at Hanover Square had established a position as the dominant force in the London orchestral world. Mara's short series that year was only a modest success.[1] At the end of the season, an urgent mission was undertaken on behalf of the Professionals by their deputy leader Borghi to attempt to repair relations with Haydn. Once again, the composer was unable to accept an offer to come to London, but it was announced that he would at least continue to send new music: 'HAYDN is not to be in London this winter, as was expected, for the purpose of composing for the Professional Concert; as long however as he continues to supply them, it will be of little consequence.'[2] The Pantheon management was not idle. It was decided to refurbish the concert arena with a view to improving the sound quality, which had attracted persistent criticism. One commentator was of the view that the building was 'not calculated for music' and that it would ideally need a band of at least 300 performers.[3] The improvements made in 1788 included a 'new Gallery over the Orchestra', 'a temporary Cieling in the Dome' and about 'Twenty Boxes round the room', all of which were to 'confine the sound'. As a result of all these alterations, the Pantheon was confidently expected to be 'the first Concert Room in Europe'.[4] But despite rumours of a new Mara series, there were no subscription concerts at the Pantheon in 1789. The Professional Concert reaped the rewards with one of its most successful seasons. The opening concert on 2 February is reported to have attracted an audience of nearly 500.[5] The proprietors of the Pantheon were clearly unhappy at the way in which events were unfolding, and the decision was taken that in 1790 a vigorous challenge must be mounted. Early reports suggested that they were bidding for the services of Haydn. The *Morning Star* on 4 July 1789 observed that continuing rivalry between the Hanover Square and Pantheon series was expected to produce 'better music than the town has heard since

---

[1]   Audiences picked up after a disappointing first concert attendance of only 260. *The Times*, 23 February 1788. McVeigh, 'The Professional Concert', 70.

[2]   *Morning Post*, 8 October 1788.

[3]   *Ibid.*, 19 November 1785. On earlier reservations over the Pantheon, see Woodfield, *Opera and Drama*, 72–4.

[4]   *Morning Post*, 30 October 1788.

[5]   McVeigh, 'The Professional Concert', 73; Francis Fowke confirms that it was 'very full' (British Library, Oriental and India Office Collections, Ormathwaite MS D 546/26, Francis Fowke to Margaret Benn, 3 February 1789).

the demise of BACH and ABEL'. Both series had as their 'great object . . . to bring over HAYDN for Composer'.

In September, the London papers began to report rumours as to who was to lead the Pantheon Grand Concert in 1790. In the *Morning Post* of 18 September, there was speculation about Giardini (who had been out of the country for six years but was looking to make a return visit), with a younger man tipped as his replacement: 'If the musical veteran GIARDINI should not venture here again, or be deemed unfit for service, Young WEICHSELL, whose talents on the violin are in the highest repute, will most probably be preferred.' Giardini was still presumed to be going to lead the Pantheon Concerts on 29 September. Then on 5 October, *The Times* made an important announcement:

THE PANTHEON

A Concert on a very enlarged and liberal scale will be the principal attraction of this elegant building the ensuing winter: it will be superior to most of the kind ever established in this country.

PACCHIEROTTI is engaged exclusively to sing at this Concert, and no other, either public or private. He is to bring with him from Italy a first woman singer, who has never yet appeared in public. His engagement is for thirteen nights, and the terms 1000 guineas.

The Concerts are to be on Thursday nights and to begin the first Thursday after the Queen's Birth-day. The music will be under the direction of Dr. BURNEY . . .

From the many known and particular admirers of *Pacchierotti* among the ladies of fashion, and the impossibility of hearing him any where else, it is probable that the Pantheon Concert will be highly in vogue.

What would have been immediately apparent to anyone reading this preliminary announcement was that the 1790 Pantheon Grand Concert was being planned as a major event. The news that Pacchierotti was to return to London was calculated to raise expectations. No other singer of Italian opera had attracted so loyal and enthusiastic a following over so long a period as he had in the early 1780s, and he was now to be marketed as an 'exclusive' attraction. With the King's Theatre in ashes and very real uncertainties over whether there would be an opera season, the timing was astute. As *The Times*'s puff clearly implies, there was every reason to believe that the Pantheon Concert would be very fashionable. For Salomon this was the most promising opportunity to have come up in London for some time. From his own experience, he could testify that newspaper gossip about who was to lead a series was often inaccurate. It perhaps occurred to him that despite the press speculation about Giardini and Weichsell he was still in with a chance, especially since the formal announcement in *The Times* had not mentioned a leader.

With the leadership of the 1790 Pantheon series apparently still an open question, Salomon went to extraordinary lengths to ingratiate himself with the Burney family. Some time early in October – the date must have been on or shortly before 6 October, since he was due in Winchester to lead the festival the following day – he called on Burney. The reason for this meeting is not known, but as Burney's role in the Pantheon Concert had just been announced, it is likely enough that he called to discuss the forthcoming series and perhaps to press his claim to the leadership. He was also there to offer his thanks for references supplied to him by Captain Phillips earlier in the year for use in Ireland. He had planned to write a letter of appreciation, but an apparently casual suggestion from Burney to the effect that he might like to express his gratitude in person seems to have been enough to ensure that Mickleham was on his itinerary. The Winchester Music Festival, advertised in the *Salisbury and Winchester Journal* as the 'Hampshire Music Meeting, 1789', took place on 7–9 October under his direction. After this engagement was over, Salomon, in the company of Joseph Reinagle (who had been principal cellist), made a number of visits in Surrey, including Farnham, where the Bishop of Winchester had his residence, and from there it was an easy journey to Mickleham.[6]

Susan Burney's extended account of Salomon's visit to her home gives us a wonderful picture of the violinist's personality and social skills. During his weekend in Surrey, he played with consummate skill and subtlety on Susan's musicality, her diffidence as a performer and her maternal pride, all of which she records with characteristic insight and honesty. There is no hint in her account that she was aware of any ulterior motive on Salomon's part, but the 'charm offensive' to which he subjected his hostess was so sustained and intense that it is hard to believe that he was not using the visit as a means of improving his standing with her father. Salomon's prospects of making a good impression had been improved by Scheener's decision to return to Switzerland with his pregnant wife. On 27 June they stopped off at her home en route to Brighthelmstone and the Continent to apologize:

Mrs Scheener *looked very blooming & pretty, but gave me a surprise* & concern by saying they could not *leave the Kingdom* without saying Adieu to us – they were going to *Geneva* – I believe they saw my regret, & quickly added *only for six weeks* – at their return they very pleasantly promised to come to us – & I sincerely hope will keep their word – Scheener asked for the Captain – mais *Helas* – I had scarce been able to *waken* him. I was much obliged to them for this little visit, & the more so as I believe they took this route merely on our account.[7]

Later Susan heard that Scheener had left his wife at Geneva 'to lie in' during her pregnancy, returning in haste to England, 'having been engaged to lead the band at Hereford Music Meeting in September'. He was still diplomatically expressing a wish to visit Mickleham after this engagement, though by now Susan had virtually given up hope of a summer visit from him. On Saturday 17 October, however, she had a

[6]   *The Letters of Charles Burney*, ed. Ribeiro, i, 381.
[7]   British Library, Egerton MS 3692, f. 14.

very pleasant surprise in the form of an unannounced visit from Salomon. The fact that he had given no prior warning at all of his intention to call is a clear enough indication that it had been hastily planned – the normal practice was to write a few days in advance so that musical plans could be made. Burney, with the Pantheon leadership in his gift and Salomon expressing interest, had perhaps used his influence to procure a musical visit for his daughter, to make up for her disappointment over the Scheeners.

To Susan's regret, the Locks were not in residence. Those present during the weekend included her husband and Esther with her teenage son Richard (who was studying the piano with Dussek) and several of her younger children, Fanny, Amelia and baby Cecilia:

Richard came here after dinner to practice – I had Norbury on my lap, at his lesson, & Fanny standing by me, when Louis came in hastely to say there was a Chaise at the door wth two Gentlemen – My heart *misgave* me – for I concluded it must be the La Trobes – Phillips however went out to the door & I soon heard a *german* sounding voice, that for a moment I thought had been *Pohlman's*[8] – but my surprise was extreme when Phillips entered in a moment, introducing – Mr Salomon. He came up to me very courteously, telling me he had lately seen my Father who had encouraged him to come to return his thanks in person to Capt. Phillips for the recommendatory letters he had given him to Ireland – these letters I know not whether I have told you – but I happened to be at my Father's last April when Mr Salomon called to tell him he had engaged himself *for 3 months* in Ireland – intimating a wish for letters if he had any Friends there – but my Father knew of no one at that time in Dublin to whom he c^d address him – Salomon then presented tickets for his benefit wch was to take place in 2 or 3 eve^{ngs} – & insisted upon *my* accepting two, for myself. Capt. P[hillips], upon my telling him what had passed in this visit, he most good humourdly said He w^d give him some letters, & accordingly wrote 3 – One to Ld Charlemont[9] – another to Dr Purcell, an eminent Physician who married a sister of Mr FitzGerald's & a 3^d to Mr Field,[10] the most famous Dillettante in Music in Dublin. Those he carried & left at Mr Salomon's lodgings, who we find had called to thank him upon the day of our leaving town, but we were already set out. When Edward was wth us He told us Salomon had lately called in Titchfield Street to enquire Capt. Phillips's direction – that he might *write to thank him* for the pleasant reception his friends had given him in Ireland – This had gratified us very much – but by no means prepared us to receive a very pleasant visit, wch w^d have made *the* amends for writing a *hundred* letters.

---

[8]   Probably Johannes Pohlman, the piano-maker whose 'charming little Instruments, sweet & even in Tone, & capable of great variety of piano & forte, between the two extremes of pianissimo and fort^{mo}', had won Burney's approval. *The Letters of Charles Burney*, ed. Ribeiro, i, 163–4. Pohlman or a relative also seems to have acted as a piano-tuner in Surrey. In a letter dated 1 June 1787, Susan Burney wrote: 'The next day came Pohlman, who tunes ours & all the pianofortes in the Neighbourhood.' Armagh Public Library, copies of 27 journal-letters from Susan to Fanny Burney, 1787–8, Letter ix.
[9]   A member of the Rotunda Music Committee. Boydell, *Rotunda Music*, 171.
[10]   Probably Robert Field, father of John Field, who played the violin in the Rotunda Band in 1783. *Ibid.*, 45.

Susan Burney continues with an appraisal of Salomon's character:

Salomon is a very well informed, sensible man, wth much [unclear], & at the same time much good humour – a very uncommon I think, quickness of parts & a great deal of wit – He is very ready in conversation – very just in his remarks & very entertaining – All this c[d] not fail to render him to Phillips an acceptable visitor, added to w[ch] He is a true enthusiast in his art, & possessed of such abilities – such feeling – fancy, fire & expression, that had he no merit but such as consisted in his musical powers, He c[d] not to me have been an unwelcome Guest.

This assessment of Salomon's personality accords well with the 'great good sense and polished manners' noted by the author of the 'Memoir'. Salomon, trained as a lawyer, usually received credit for being well educated and widely read. His company was valued by scientists such as William Herschell and Joseph Banks, the latter, 'not having the slightest taste for music', appreciating Salomon for his 'social qualities and mental attainments'.[11] He was a highly accomplished linguist, writing and speaking four languages 'with astonishing correctness and fluency'. Susan Burney noted his German accent, but she reports his conversation as full of fashionable French social idioms. What is missed in the published 'Memoir' and what Susan Burney captures so vividly is Salomon's quiet sense of humour, his willingness to make fun of pomposity.

The formalities were quickly over, Salomon having introduced his companion, Reinagle the cellist, who had been engaged at Winchester and who was with Salomon, Susan assumed, only to provide him with a reliable bass line.[12] The remainder of the evening (accommodation having been offered to the visitors after a tentative inquiry about the local inn) was taken up with conversation and music:

Whilst he was paying his Comp[ts] to me, Phillips returned to the other Gentleman, who soon followed in. It was a M[r] Renaigle [Reinagle – Susan's spelling is inconsistent] – a Violoncello Player many years ago recommended by Corri to my Father but whom I had never before seen. He is a middle aged, foreign looking Man, but I believe a Scotchman – at least he had resided there *16 years* he s[d] before he came to England, a rather simple sort of Person – & not very *high bred* in manners, Salomon we found had been visiting Farnham, & in other parts of Surry, wth this Gent[m] of whom I conceive it was not very easy for him to *se defaire* even [if] he wished it – but indeed wherever he goes, unless he finds a good Harps[d] Player to accompany him, the having a *certain base* must be very necessary.

He spoke highly of Richard's improvements, having very lately heard him in Titchfield Street – but I hurried him off for my Sister, who had not purposed coming out that eve[g]. Salomon made enquiries concerning our *Inn* – but I was

11   Anon., 'Memoir', 47.
12   In Highfill, Burnim and Langhans, *A Biographical Dictionary*, xii, 305–6, Joseph Reinagle, described as the principal cellist in the Salomon Concerts under Haydn 1791–2, is stated to have 'had the honor of enjoying Haydn's intimate acquaintance & friendship & rec[d] many serviceable hints on composition from that great Master'. The source is not given. Reinagle is not listed as one of the cellists in Salomon's own advertisement. See Landon, *Haydn in England*, 131.

very glad we had our two beds unoccupied, wch enabled us to beg that He & his friend w^d seek for no other house for this night – & it was not long unsettled that they w^d stay with us till Monday. I truly regretted that this unexpected treat had not presented itself when M^r & Mrs Lock were at Norbury – & Indeed had it happened when M^r B & Edward were here, as was the case the preceding Saturday, it w^d have given us as perfect a Quartetto as c^d have been desired – For my *own* part however, it w^d have been most unreasonable to have murmur'd – Since tho' this regale might have been heightened, it was yet so unexpected & Delightful.

The Instruments (2 *fiddles* & a violoncello) presently were bro^t in by Louis to *gladden my sight* – While Salomon took great notice of our *Family* – 'they are like two little *angels* – en verité – mais – ce sont *des chefs d'oeuvres!* – On ne voit pas des Enfans comme ceux las!' Norbury was full of curiosity about the Instruments – but still more comically struck by the *names* – He always called one of these Gentlemen Mr *Solo*mon very emphatically & sometimes adding – *that is so wise* & Mr Reneigle reminded him of Mithridates, of whom Fanny has lately been reading in Mrs Trimmer's book, whose name he calls thus Mr *Redates* – 'I am very glad' s^d he to me 'that Gentleman is Mr *Reneigle*, & not Mr *Redates* because Mr *Redates* was such a *wicked* man!'

Salomon gave a very entertaining & characteristic acc^t of the reception he met in Ireland – chiefly dwelling upon *Phillips's* Friends – of Ld Charlemont's *courteous* behaviour etc etc – He knew our friend[s] Miss[es] Kirwans there, & said they had enquired anxiously after *toute la Famille Burney* – In the midst of this acc^t wch he made very entertaining & interesting, arrived my Sister – not less surprised than I had been – wth her Boy & Girl – We had then some general conversation & Tea – & after it Salomon was as good humourdly ready to promote our having music, as anybody in the party c^d be to listen to it. Richard first played a lesson of Dussecks – during wch in the midst of much praise & encouragement Salomon made some excellent critiques – wch I think were he a little older he might much profit from – but at present whatever he thinks like Dusseck[13] seems to him perfect – & it is a natural error, & whilst he has any

[13] Dussek, fleeing from the French Revolution, arrived in London in the summer of 1789. He quickly became a favourite of Charles and Esther Burney at Titchfield Street. Susan was informed by Marianne her niece that 'M Dussec – a great Piano Forte player, who to my great Satisfaction has excited a most unexpected degree of emulation in Richard who is I understand wonderfully improved of late – Mr Dussec is likewise a favourite wth Mr B. & my sister for his unassuming & unaffected manners, & the Girls are raving about him as the most handsome & accomplished man they have seen – but fortunately *Fanny* is the most desperately in love – Marianne only laughs, & admires wth moderation.' British Library, Egerton MS 3692, f. 73. 'His improvement in his P. F. playing was really almost wonderful since I had heard him in town – wch was not above half a year before – but bears date *much* within that time – & has been in great part the work of Mr Dussek – whose instructions, wch do much honour to the liberality & good nature of the Master, have not been uselessly bestowed on the Scholar. I had heard much of his improvement yet was astonished at it – Much to the pleasure of Edward – who is very sincerely interested in the progress he makes – & Either wth much endeavour expresses these obligations to this young man for his voluntary assistance in stimulating Rich^d to excell himself. I think he will make a very great Player in a style wholly different from that of either his father or mother – who *in* that style he w^d certainly never equal – His manner is perfectly *foreign* – & has many great beauties & some defects – but I have not time just now to enter into a *critique raisonnée* – What I have s^d will however I am sure give pleasure to my dearest Fanny.' British Library, Egerton MS 3692, f. 101^v.

probability of gaining from him new instructions, may even be a useful one. Salomon's critique judiciously & I thought kindly, was addressed to his mother – I felt the truth of every word he uttered – & I believe his eyes, frequently, & quickly glancing my way, made him soon aware that I agreed wth him.

He afterwards accomp^d Richard in a beautiful lesson of Kozeluch's to wch he did not indeed do justice – having lately practiced no music but Dusseck's – His mother after this took his place, & till supper appeared, regaled me wth a variety of exquisite lessons in wch Salomon accomp^d her most delightfully.

It was a treat! – to make me some amends I supposed, *providentially*, for *Scheener's defection* – Who so long, & so vainly we had hoped to see here & who I really believe *wished* to have kept his word but that – '*his lot forbade*' – He c^d not I conclude *prudently* have left London – & he is too good I believe to act imprudently – nor I am sure ought we to wish him to gratify us at such an expence.

Our supper was very pleasant – Salomon pleased wth the pleasure he had given – & all else wth that they had rec^d. When Esther & her young ones went home, I retired – but was not of a great while indeed followed by Phillips, who was induced to talk of the Sandwich Islands etc wch so amused & interested Salomon, that they did not part till after one in the morning.[14]

Susan Burney's rather pointed comment on the 'defection' of Scheener shows just how delicate a matter it was for a professional musician to refuse the offer of a private visit on the grounds of a public obligation. Scheener's inability to visit Surrey had not caused a rift with the Burneys, but many would have been less understanding.

The following day was to be given over to music-making. Salomon had already heard Esther and Richard Burney, but he had not yet succeeded in persuading his host to play. He now did so with masterly tact:

The next day Sunday October 18th I rose early intending to arrange all my domestic affairs before breakfast in wch I was so happy as to succeed – The Gentⁿ had over night plan'd to go up Box Hill – but the morn^g was wet, & Richard who was to have called for them did not come – During breakfast the conversation was chiefly upon the South Sea Isands, wch Mr Renaigle laughably enough seemed to be desperately anxious to visit – tho' ill prepared, indeed perfectly ignorant as to the difficulty he must in such a case be destined to undergo – It made some very ridiculous talk – wch I am sorry the hurry of the time in wch it passed prevented my minuting down & so long after I remember nothing distinctly.

As soon as the Breakfast aparatus was removed, Mr Salomon, who had *gently* asked me to *Play* the preceding eve^g, & who very sensibly was soon quieted by my manner of declaring incapacity, renewed this request, but tho' not wth *violence*, wth very persevering persuasion – always unlucky upon these occasions, my *constitutional* terrors were increased, by knowing myself out of practice, not having even touched a note since the arrival of my sister – or rather

[14]   As a lieutenant, Phillips had sailed on Cook's last expedition. Hemlow, *The History of Fanny Burney*, 142.

since I knew her intention of coming. My difficulties in practicing are such, that greatly as I love Music, I require now the stimulus of having our Friends up the Hill to require my playing, to incite me to get thro' them & when I knew Esther was coming, I depended on a long Holyday – Mr Salomon however persisted – & being joined by Phillips, I knew defence w^d be in vain – He saw however how much I was frightened, & after urging all kinds of persuasion, he added, 'When a Lady is *so modeste* as Mrs Phillips – so *very* diffident – *believe me criticism w^d be disarmed* even were there a *wish* to be severe – but – you cannot fail to please *me* – for it *must* give me pleasure – if only to see you – *there*' – pointing significantly to the P. Forte – I knew his flattering meaning – & I will be conceited enough to add that I believe I was Long ago marked out by this Gentleman as one who listened with feeling to Music – & whom he therefore concluded w^d not do anything *very* shocking, tho' no capital Performer. However the better his opinion of me – the greater my fear – but having made my apology as well as I c^d – at length I sate down – but rejected Pleyell who was on the desk, as too difficult to play when frightened & took a Lesson of Schroeter's.

Throughout the first movement he s^d all he c^d to encourage me – how well it went etc etc – & made me repeat both Parts – The 2^d movement is quick – but notwithstanding, my fright subsiding in a degree – My very good natured & flattering accompanier exclaimed as if *cela lui echappoit* upon some passage that I suppose I executed better than he expected – 'Upon my Word – You surprise me!' – However I almost surprised myself wth playing so ill – fortunately there was a 3^d movement wch is easy & rather slow – & in this I was more able to command myself – & *to be sincere*, encouraged as I c^d not but find myself by Salomon's manner, & flattering expressions, I did not disgrace myself so much as usual when I have any listeners – 'But – you play *Charmingly*', cried Salomon – & expressed so much surprise – & – I really must say *pleasure* – strange as even to myself it seems to recollect it – that I really think it a mercy it did not turn my head, & make me unable to finish the movement.

When it was over – He said *such* things – to Phillips more than to me – as wth all my *Amour propre*, wch I confess was brought a little into play on this occasion, I c^d not possibly repeat – But what *touched* me the more, because I believe it was sincere, was his lamentation that wth *un si beau naturel* as he was pleased to express himself, I had not given a great deal of time in my Childhood to the vanquishing of difficulties – in wch case – selon lui – Mrs Phillips would have played – *better than anybody*!! rien que cela ma chere – qu'en pensy vous!

He really seemed a little *Frantic* on the occasion – but his great good nature so far dispelled my fear of him that I *suffered myself to be persuaded* to play another lesson, wch I knew very superficially – but he had set his heart on playing it with me – & tho' I knew it far less perfectly than the first I had attempted, having so much more courage, I played it better – & nothing c^d be more flattering than Mr Salomon – & – the Infection was caught by poor Mr Reinagle – who then tho^t *he* c^d discover that *Mrs Phillips was a great genius*.

I was hearing these unmerited Comp^{ts} when Richard came in – how I rejoiced he had not made his appearance whilst I was at the Instrument! – the rain had ceased – but instead of going up Box Hill, my Captain took his Gentlemen to see Norbury. Soon after they were gone My sister came wth Fanny & then Augusta & Amelia, whose comp^y I had beg'd to dinner, tho' before I knew the great treat I sh^d have to give them – They were you will suppose –

much pleased – but we lamented anew that Mr Salomon had chosen this Sunday to come to us when M^r & Mrs Lock were absent.

He came back delighted with Norbury – My sister was at the P. Forte, playing unaccomp^d lessons to wch he listened with great pleasure – always in a very flattering manner turning to me at the passages he most delighted in.

During dinner, Reinagle demonstrated himself socially less cultivated than his colleague, and afterwards, when some time was spent in amusing the children, his playing of a solo caused some unintended amusement:

Thus passed the time till we were summoned to dinner, during wch Salomon was very lively & amusing, & all went well – except in *one instance* – wch was his mistaking my toast & water for some *sweet wine*, and pouring himself out a Glass, & inviting Mr Reinagle at the same time to drink wth him – but no sooner had he got it in his mouth than he too late perceived his *unfortunate mistake* – & the difficulty he was under – to prevent laughing – & to swallow a beverage wch I find none like but those who use themselves to no other, first caught my attention, & made me discover the *error* he had committed – tho' doubtless *disappointed*, he was not discomposed by this mistake, but laughed very heartily at it – Whilst Mr Reinagle made me more inclined to laugh by the solemnity wth which he felicitated himself upon not having accepted his invitation to drink wth him.

At Desert we had the sweet little Cecilia – & my quiet little Fanny, & riotous Norbury – & with these, having satisfied their *demands*, we Females came up stairs – & the Dear Girls, who doat upon a *Baby* s^d *Cecilia* was quite *adorable*, & kept her between them till it was time for nurse to carry her home.

We were soon after joined by the Gentlemen – & so delightfully ready was Salomon to make the most of the evening that he began immediately, & played a beautiful Set of Pleyell's Trios, containing 3, thro' before tea appeared – These he played wth such spirit, feeling, & energy, that it was indeed a most delightful performance. Mr Reinagle played the tenor part exceedingly well & our Esther the Base on the Piano Forte.

We had then Tea – & during this Mr Reinagle was good natured enough to take out his Violoncello to gratify Norbury, & played him a *literal* Solo – that is a solo in wch he had no accomp^t but what he gave himself – He is reckoned by some the best Violoncello we have after Cervetto & Crosdill – but it was however a desperately rough performance, & I scarce dared look towards Salomon or Esther during it – having once accidentally caught a glance of the former, I was almost undone – & it was most happy that I sate out of the poor man's sight – who was likewise I believe too profoundly engaged in his laborious performance to observe anybody during it – It seemed at first almost to stun & stupify even Norbury – but having stood aghast a little time, he seemed to have had full & sufficient gratification of his curiosity – & walked off to another part of the room, to observe upon something else – The solo having been proposed for *his* amusement, the effect was very ridiculous, tho' perfectly natural – Had I not had full employment in making Tea, I sh^d certainly have undertaken to keep him by the Performer, & as quiet as I c^d during his performance – but this I c^d not attempt – nor depute any one else, because it w^d the more strongly have marked, how little Mr Renaigle succeeded in amusing him.

After tea our ears were healed by Kozeluch,[15] charmingly played by Esther, & admirably accomp^d by the indefatigable Salomon – they played a great number of delicious lessons – then Richard gave a Dusseck – & last Mr Salomon played over 3 or 4 beautiful (at least as ^he played them) Pieces of his own, in wch Reinagle accomp^d him on the Violoncello – It was a truly delightful musical evening – I forgot to mention that immediately after the Trios Mr Salomon in the most courteous & persuasive manner applied to me to let him accomp^y me again in the lessons we had tried in the morn^g – I was ashamed that Esther sh^d stand by & hear him & She I believe was surprised too – Salamon seemed astonished that *She* sh^d not have heard me, & said in a tone of concern what, if *anything*, c^d, w^d have carried me to the P. F. – '*Oh! – She has played to you sometime – & you have not encouraged her!*' – You may conceive how warmly I deffended my partial & kind Esther from this charge – & He then had the goodness to say a great deal to her of the same flattering kind concerning my *naturel* as he called it, as he had said to my Capt & Mr Renaigle in the morn^g.

La Bonne came for the dear Girls, & heard one piece – They went away before our supper, wch tho' we were almost *exhausted* by pleasure & attention, was very pleasant. It is impossible to say what Friends Mr Salomon & I are – & Mr Reinagle *took as much* to my Captain – I cannot say he had *the better bargain* – he threatened him hard wth future visits.

After Esther and her young ones were gone, I was detained a little while to hear Salomon & Mr Renaigle try over a motet of Mich^l Wise's from my Father's Hist^y.[16] Salomon's method of directing Renaigle in it, tho' very good humoured, was so comically cavalier that tho' it is a very fine composition, I c^d not help laughing till I was almost ashamed throughout it.

Mr Renaigle is as great an admirer of Scotch music as poor Mr B. [?] used to be – & no less impenetrable & positive in argument – Salomon's method of laughing at him upon this subject was extremely humourous & comical – sans

[15] The fashionable piano music studied by Burney's daughters in the late 1780s consisted of sonatas and accompanied sonatas by Haydn, Pleyel, Kozeluch, Schröter and, after 1789, Dussek. Their reaction to Kozeluch illuminates an interesting moment in the reception history of German/Viennese/Bohemian instrumental music in England. For a short period, the music of Kozeluch was readily equated with that of Haydn and by some even preferred to it. Susan Burney spent the evening of 28 May 1789 at Norbury Park with the Locks: 'The eve^g was deliciously spent in Music & I have the gratification of finding Kozeluch *triumphant over all prejudices* – for at first hearing his music there was the strongest inclination to run it down – nobody had any merit but *Haydn* – How apt we are to be a little bigoted – Haydn is now more likely to be *turned wholly out*, from Norbury, for Kozeluch, than he ever w^d by *me* – for I love & delight in both.' British Library, Egerton MS 3692, f. 35^v. While Susan Burney maintained an even-handed attitude to the two composers, her friend Mrs Lock displayed the exaggerated preference that was so often the hallmark of fashionable attitudes to composers. On 14 October, Susan again visited Norbury: 'In the eve^ng I accomp^d Esther to Norbury – We took Richard with us – who played two lessons – but his style was too new to be thoroughly tasted by our dear Mrs Lock – who in *music*, seems generally to require some use before she enjoys great pleasure. So Kozeluch at first was heard *a peine*, & barely tolerated – & now Kozeluch *alone* seems to be perfectly enjoyed. I who admire him beyond all other P. Forte Composers am nevertheless vexed at a predeliction pushed so far, as almost continually to set aside all other composers – even the great Haydn himself.' British Library, Egerton MS 3692, f. 103. To judge by the number of Kozeluch's pieces that Salomon included in his Hanover Square series with Haydn, he too was an admirer.
[16] Wise's anthem *The Ways of Zion*, highly praised by Burney, is in *A General History*, ed. Mercer, ii, 357–9. It is for treble and bass voices and continuo.

jamais descoutee his antagonist – who seldom understood above half his meaning.

On the morning of his departure, Salomon continued to woo Susan Burney, complimenting her on her musicality (rather than her playing ability), giving general advice on practice and adroitly qualifying this when the impossibility of a young mother combining domestic responsibilities with serious practice was raised:

Monday Octr 19th we had a very pleasant breakfast during wch Mr Salomon made us a promise of a future visit – 'Were it earlier in the year' s^d he, 'I sh^d *decree* it for this year – but the winter advances quick, & so I must hope to repeat this *great* pleasure to *myself*, next summer. He s^d a thousand polite & pleasant things of the satisfaction the visit had procured him. He enquired Fanny's age, & seemed surprised to find I had so long been married. 'Oh', said he very drolly – 'had I been so fortunate as to know – you – & your *talents* – before that time – indeed – I w^d not have *let you alone*' – meaning he w^d have made me *practice* – He had before told me if I w^d practice *two hours* a day for *two years*, I sh^d do *anything what ever* I pleased on the P. F. My manner of hearing him, as he is very quick, convinced him of what an impossible thing he was advising – to a wife – & a mother – He afterwards wth flattering sort of interest gave me more feasible advice – to play *easy* music – '& then' he added, 'you will play it – as *nobody else plays it*'.

He certainly had determined to turn my head if he c^d with vanity. He recommended to me a lesson of Hulmandel's wch has a similarly beautiful motion – I have since got it.

He made many enquiries after *Miss Burney at Windsor* [Fanny Burney] – if she loved music etc. etc.

Our breakfast was but just over when – Rich^d came – & Phillips joined the Gent^n in a walk up Box Hill. Before they returned home they stop'd to visit my Sister, & found the Chaise wh^{ch} was to carry them to London at the door – during their absence I had written to my dear Father, & I gave my letter to Mr Salomon, who had previously told me he sh^d see him on business as soon as he sh^d get to town. He & Mr Renaigle took a short repast before they set out, & left us much delighted by the visit, & seeming little less so themselves.

It may be significant that Salomon was expecting to see Burney 'on business', perhaps to get a response to a bid for the Pantheon leadership, the moment he reached London again.

When Susan Burney returned to London later in the autumn, Scheener, back from Hereford, seized his chance to make amends for his failure to visit Mickleham. She heard good news of his future prospects:

Mr Scheener called, & readily accepted the invitation to join us ... he ... most good naturedly offered to play or accomp^y anything from that time till 8 in the evening – you may imagine this proposal was not *cooly* accepted – Indeed I saw his intention was to gratify me, & I felt truely obliged to him. I made many enquiries after his pretty wife – & was pleased in observing the pleasure my enquiries gave him & the affection wth wch he spoke of her. He purposes going over for her in May – He gave me an acc^t of the hindrances he had met in his wishes of coming to Mickleham – some of them gave me pleasure – as I hope they will be serviceable to him – among these was his having been noticed by the D. of Dorset, who, for some time has had him once or twice a week to play Trios & quartettos wth him – As I believe he is a liberal Patron, this gave me real pleasure to hear.[17]

Very soon after dinner we all went into the Drawing room, & from half past 4 till near 8 o'clock Scheener played – exquisitely – & in the manner the most obliging & delightful – He evidently tho' little *i* alone was his Hearer, played w[th] *care*, & in his most polished & deliciously pathetic manner – He played several of Haydn's Quartettos, & accomp[d] Esther in 3 delightful pieces of Kozeluch, & when we had tea, & M[r] B ran away to his engagement, he seemed wth real reluctance to take leave – as wth true regrets we saw him go – He is a very pleasing & I believe excellent young man – I am very sorry we can so seldom hope to see him.

Scheener did in fact retain his contacts with the Burney family in London. In 1791, he was included by Haydn in his list of violinists in the 'First London Notebook'.[18] In the autumn of 1795, Susan Burney again heard him at her sister's house: 'In the eve[g] M[r] *Scheener* came in, w[ch] was not very unfortunate for me, & I heard a quite new set of lessons of Haydn played over by Esther accomp[d] by the above named exquisite performer.'[19]

Salomon, meanwhile, had by no means finished his campaign to ingratiate himself with the Burneys. Susan heard from her niece that he had been singing her praises to an almost embarrassing extent:

Before I left town my sister had a visit from D[r] *Huett* – a very *musical medecin* & a passionate admirer of Salomon's – his conversation was almost wholly relating to him – & this brings to mind something concerning *that* admirable performer in w[ch] I am too much interested not to be tempted to communicate it – Soon after he visited Titchfield Street, & met wth Marianne [Esther's eldest child] alone, who made him tea, & whom he persuaded to play to him after it – He was very good natured & encouraging to her – but – what much more *surprised* me, made M[rs] Phillips the chief topic of his discourse, & *her musical talents* – s[d] to Marianne many of the same very flattering things he had before said here on this *extraordinary subject* – concluding by these words – 'I have not – *I assure you, heard anybody play with so much feeling of a great while'* – This acc[t] surprised *at least* as much as it gratified me – & that is not saying a *little* neither – but it did not do me much good – tempting me to useless regret that La Madre rendered early improvement by regular practice impossible – & even that the power of keeping up the little I am able to do in music sh[d] frequently be attended wth such difficulty – In such cases I can only end wth the *useful saying* that '*it will all be the same a hundred years hence*'! & so *Je me console*.

I charged Marianne, for various reasons, w[ch] I did not unfold to her, to keep

---

[17] The Duke of Dorset was a noted patron of musicians. McVeigh, *Concert Life*, 36.

[18] Landon, *Haydn in England*, 183.

[19] Armagh Public Library, copies of 52 journal-letters from Susan to Fanny Burney, 1795–9, Letter xv, 3 November 1795. This set of 'lessons' was probably either Hob. XV/21–3, *Trois sonates pour le piano forte, avec accompagnement de violon & violoncelle* (London: Preston & Son, [1795]); or Hob. XV/24–6, *Trois sonates pour le piano forte, avec accompagnement de violon & violoncelle* (London: Longman & Broderip, [1795]).

this *extravagant compliment* of Salomon's *a profound secret* – & tho' she was diverted by my earnestness, I hope she will mind the injunction – *You* cannot fail guessing who I chiefly feared might be a little offended & even *hurt* by a praise so expressed & wch I assure you in me creates as much astonishment as it c^d in most other persons.

Susan clearly recognized that the chief obstacle to her musical progress would remain the burden of domestic responsibilities.

The mixture of social deference and personal warmth which characterized the relationship between male professional and female amateur commonly found its expression in extravagant flattery of the kind given by both Scheener and Salomon. However, in any reading of Susan Burney's account of the behaviour of the two men, Salomon comes across as more urgent and intense than Scheener – 'frantic', as she on one occasion described him. It is of course possible that his visit to Mickleham was a routine courtesy call as he was passing through the neighbourhood, yet the coincidence of dates is very striking. If his weekend in Surrey did form part of a bid for the Pantheon leadership, his behaviour might be seen as a reflection of the intensity with which he was seeking the position and, by implication, of the importance he attached to winning it.

If Salomon was hoping that his relationship with the Burneys would be the decisive factor in winning him the appointment, he was to be disappointed. Only two weeks after his return to London on 19 October, news of Weichsell's appointment was announced. The reason given for the choice of a younger player (probably aimed at Giardini as well as himself) can hardly have been taken by him as a good omen for the future:

Young WEICHSELL, whose abilities as a performer on the Violin, are so highly celebrated, is engaged to lead the Concerts at the Pantheon. It is not for the sake of novelty that this young man is preferred to the veteran performers now in this country; but because no veteran performer is to be considered as his superior, so that he brings with equal talents all the fire of juvenile enthusiasm.[20]

That it had been Burney's decision is made abundantly clear: 'Dr. BURNEY has the entire regulation of the Pantheon Concerts, and where could a person of more taste, judgement, and liberal decorum, be found for such a task?' As the autumn progressed, it became ever clearer that Salomon had missed a key opportunity to compete with Cramer. The *Morning Post* of 15 December announced that the Pantheon intended to have a 'vigorous conflict' with the Professional Concert 'to try which will be most successful in gaining the patronage of the higher circles'. The Professional Concert was reported to be considering measures to hinder the rival organization:

[20]   *Morning Post*, 31 October 1789. McVeigh, *Concert Life*, 86.

By the Articles of the Professional Concert, it seems, that the members are precluded from playing at any other concert, except the Pantheon, which is specially favoured. It is now said that the Professional Concert, beginning to think the Pantheon likely to become too formidable a rival, have determined to include the Pantheon in the prohibition.

If the result of this were to be 'a spirit of opposition', it was hoped that 'emulation' would be 'inflamed', equal to the Handel–Bononcini conflict. Having been relegated to the sidelines, Salomon now entered an association with the Academy of Ancient Music, an organization of rising status, but one that could hardly be said to have the prestige of the main subscription series.[21]

---

[21]   McVeigh, *The Violinist*, 33. Again, Cramer, leading the Concert of Ancient Music, had the more prestigious position. Salomon, however, had the 'consolation' of leading at Lady Yonge's private concert on alternate weeks. McVeigh, *Concert Life*, 47.

6

Salomon and the Revival of the Italian Cantata

Salomon's failure to win the Pantheon leadership left his fortunes seemingly at a low ebb, but behind the scenes he had renewed his contact with Haydn. In a remarkable change of fortune, this would enable him within a year to establish a position as a major player in the London orchestral world. A warm relationship with the composer had been established with the assistance of his associate John Bland, who visited Haydn late in 1789 with a view to purchasing new chamber works.[1] Salomon was also in the market for new works, very probably in the expectation of being able to present them at the Pantheon. In a letter to Bland dated 12 April 1790, Haydn informed him that in addition to the remaining piano trios he had agreed to supply, he would send 'a brand new and very beautiful cantata for Herr Salomon'. The composer asked Bland to present Salomon with his most sincere compliments, thanking him for his proposed fee of 40 ducats, and promising to send him also 'a brand new and magnificent symphony'. The cantata was for the voice of 'my dear Storace, whom I kiss many times'.[2] Bland himself was promised another cantata, *Ariadne*, once it had been orchestrated. The information in this letter suggests that despite the long-standing English interest in Haydn's symphonies on the part of London orchestras, and the desire of music-sellers to obtain new chamber works such as quartets and piano trios, a different genre altogether, the Italian solo cantata, was coming to the fore in dealings between the composer and his English contacts.

As so often in questions concerning contemporary Italian vocal repertoire, Burney comes across behind the scenes as an active arbiter of taste as well as a reporter of it. In this instance, there are reasons for believing that he was directly involved in an attempt to revive the fortunes of a genre which was by now not often heard in England. His critique of contemporary music in the last volumes of *A General History of Music* (1789) ends with a brief consideration of the Italian cantata. He singles out for praise Sarti's settings of Metastasio's 'charming little poems', and the reason is immediately apparent: 'these exquisite compositions were produced ... expressly for the voices of Pacchiarotti,

[1] Woodfield, 'John Bland', 223.
[2] H. C. Robbins Landon, 'Four New Haydn Letters', *Haydn Yearbook*, 13 (1982), 213–19; 'More Haydn Letters in Autograph', *Haydn Yearbook*, 14 (1983), 200–5. See also *idem*, 'Zu den Haydn-Autographen der Sammlung Paul Sacher', *Komponisten des 20. Jahrhunderts in der Paul Sacher Stiftung* (Basle, 1986), 31–6.

Marchesi, and Rubinelli', the castrati Burney most admired. He regretted that such pieces were not more widely known in England:

Indeed, it is to be lamented that a species of composition so admirably calculated for concerts as the *cantata*, should now be so seldom cultivated: as it contains a little drama entire, having a beginning, a middle, and an end, in which the charms of poetry are united with those of Music, and the mind is amused while the ear is gratified. Opera scenes, or single songs, now supply the place of cantatas in all private concerts; but, besides the loss which these sustain when taken out of their niche, as they were originally calculated for a numerous orchestra, they can seldom be completely accompanied by a small band.[3]

Burney here makes a clear distinction between the cantata – a complete composition – and the operatic *scena*. It is interesting that his chief objection to the latter was its poetic rather than its musical incompleteness. As he implies, single songs and scenas were very popular in fashionable concerts during the 1780s. Indeed, this repertoire had been the basis for the Gallini–Cramer partnership, which promoted leading Italian opera stars at the Hanover Square subscription concert series. Italian opera songs had also formed the core repertoire of his own private concerts as far back as the days of Millico. As he knew from his own experience, one disadvantage of such pieces in the context of private performance was that the scoring sometimes needed to be reduced. Burney's plea was thus for the development of the Italian cantata, the genre best calculated to display the talents of star castrati like Pacchierotti in concerts, private and public.

In the light of Burney's public support for the revival of this genre, Salomon's highly unusual choice of a cantata for his 1789 benefit looks very unlike a coincidence. The composer of the unsuccessful work was Vincenzo Federici, whose ballet *Annette et Lubin* had received its première at the King's Theatre a few days earlier. A lesser man, having emptied a concert room with the assistance of a 'monotonous and lugubre' cantata, might have abandoned the genre altogether. Salomon's response – and again one detects the advice of Burney – was to approach Haydn for an original work with which to repair his reputation. Beneath his polished and deferential exterior, Salomon was evidently a man of some determination.

To judge by the date of Haydn's letter to Bland, Salomon is unlikely to have received his new cantata in time to be performed during the 1790s season. Its first public performance in London was thus perhaps at the third concert of his 1791 series, at which Nancy Storace (the singer for whom Haydn had written the piece) performed a 'new cantata' by the composer. The identity of the piece is unclear. It has been suggested that it was *Miseri noi, misera patria*, which was composed in or before 1790.[4] This survives in two versions, one of which does indeed appear

---

3   Burney, *A General History*, ed. Mercer, ii, 638.
4   Landon, *Haydn in England*, 62.

to be a rescored version for use in London. H. C. Robbins Landon, however, suggests the alternative possibility of the much earlier *Ah, come il cor*, published by Artaria as a cantata in 1783. Burney himself had persuaded Pacchierotti to sing it in 1783, possibly unaware that the piece was from an opera, Artaria's title page describing it as a 'Cantata per un Soprano con Accompagnamento'. This was perhaps the unspecified piece advertised by Longman & Broderip in 1788: 'A Favorite Italian Cantata with Accompaniments for a Band, composed by Sig^r Haydn'.[5] Certainly *Arianna a Naxos* can be ruled out as Salomon's piece, because Haydn specifically promised to send it to Bland once it had been orchestrated.

A Haydn cantata was performed at a private concert arranged by Lady Clarges on 31 March 1790, to which the Burneys were invited:

I spent all of the morn^g that I c^d with my Fanny … Phillips & I were carried by my dear Father to L^y Clarges's – We were amongst the first, & immediately greeted by Pacchierotti – L^y Cl: told me I had not lost a note of him – but that he w^d have his rubber at Whist before he c^d be got to sing, so she added she w^d get it over as fast as she c^d …

Pacchierotti sung three songs – one of which was encored – & not I think the best, wch was that he began with – a very fine Cantata of Haydn's, in a grand style & wch he sung exquisitely – the 2^d was a song of Hasse's, wch Tenducci used to sing when first in England – a sweet tho' old fashioned air – Pacchierotti was playful, fanciful & charming in it – & this he was prevailed on to repeat, much to the satisfaction of L^y Mary, by whom it had been chosen – his last was an air of not much expression or novelty by Guglielmi – of wch however he made as much as was possible.[6]

Whatever the identity of the composition, it perfectly answered Burney's desire to hear Italian cantatas sung by a leading castrato. When Haydn came to London, he brought with him as promised (but unorchestrated) the cantata *Arianna*. He published it himself in association with John Bland. The piece was a huge success, especially with English amateurs. Burney sent a copy of the work to Susan at Mickleham:

Wednesday 23 March 1791

My dear Father has sent me a beautiful Cantata of Haydn's, the subject is Ariadne betrayed & forsaken by Theseus – Norbury was extremely desirous of understanding the words, & at last I told him & Fanny the story, translating a part of the poetry – It affected my poor Boy most sensibly, tho' he made the most manly efforts restrain his tears – 'Theseus was a cruel wretch!' he exclaimed – '*killing wild beasts when he was like a wild beast himself to poor Ariadne!*' – his emotion was so great, that I was obliged to think of twenty ridiculous stories to tell him before I let him go to bed, to drive the impression from his mind. Yesterday in the midst of the most folâtre gaiety it occur'd to him again – He

[5] *Morning Post*, 30 October 1788.
[6] New York Public Library, Berg Collection, Susanna E. B. Phillips, holograph diary for 1786–92.

asked me if *Mrs Billington* c^d sing *that song about poor Ariadne, of Haydn's*? 'Yes', I said – & that she had been singing such songs at Dublin – 'Oh!', cried he, looking horror'd – '*I am afraid she will be killed by the Irish Savages!*' Where he took such an idea I have not the least conception – I defended the Irish *de mon mieux*, assuring him there were no *Savages* there – & Fanny, to assist me, s^d to him, 'What would Papa say if he was to hear you talk of there being *Savages in Ireland?*' 'Why, What can the Irish Savages be to Papa?', cried the little person rolling himself on the carpet, & looking very comical & at his ease – 'He was *born* in Ireland indeed – but then he went away when he was *but only a little child*, & didn't go to it any more, till he was *a great tall man – like Mr Packarotte, the Roman!*'[7]

When all the pertinent facts are put together – Burney's published plea for more chamber cantatas, Salomon's unsuccessful attempt to please his benefit audience with a cantata, Haydn's letter promising cantatas to both Salomon and Bland, and Pacchierotti's performance of a Haydn cantata at Lady Clarges's concert – a picture emerges of a systematic attempt to revive the Italian chamber cantata in England, through the popularizing of examples by Haydn. Burney comes across as an active promoter of a genre he favoured.

---

[7] New York Public Library, Berg Collection, Susanna E. B. Phillips, holograph diary for 1786–92.

7

The 1790 Concert Season

The London concert world in the spring of 1790 was in a vibrant but uncertain state. The cataclysm that had struck on the night of 17 June 1789 when the King's Theatre burned down had yet to be fully resolved. As a temporary expedient, Gallini decided to stage a season of Italian opera at the Little Theatre in the Haymarket. His partnership with Cramer remained intact,[1] and the Hanover Square subscription series once again had the benefit of Marchesi's services. In contrast to the previous year, a re-invigorated Pantheon with its star, Pacchierotti, was now providing much stronger competition.

When Susan Burney arrived in London for her traditional spring visit, the two main subscription series led by Cramer and Weichsell were in full flow. Salomon's future was looking distinctly uncertain. His career was hardly yet irretrievably lost, but ominous warning signs were there. Cramer was now undisputed as London's top leader, directing the three most prestigious ensembles, the King's Theatre orchestra, the Professional Concert and the Concert of Ancient Music. Weichsell's appointment as leader of the Pantheon series added to the pool of potential leaders a young violinist of high calibre. Still more worrying was the arrival of Giornovichi, and newspapers were even starting to speculate about the plans of Viotti. Despite his appointment as leader of the Academy of Ancient Music, Salomon was clearly in danger of losing the status he had enjoyed (after Giardini's departure) as Cramer's chief rival. Had he not been able to re-establish himself at the head of a major concert series, there must have been the real possibility that his career as a top leader in London would have been effectively over. During her stay in London, Susan Burney heard the four violinists (Salomon, Weichsell, Giardini and Giornovichi) who now might be thought the leading contenders to take on Cramer, and her comments make for interesting comparisons.

On the evening of 14 March, she renewed her acquaintance with Scheener, who was at Titchfield Street with the composer Gyrowitz and Miss Abrams, long an associate of Salomon's. Much though she continued to appreciate his playing, the Swiss violinist was obviously not in the running for any major London position. Two days later she attended Miss Abrams's benefit concert, at which Salomon was playing:

---

[1] The *Morning Post* on 29 September 1789 reported: 'CRAMER is so excellent a performer, that GALLINI is very wisely unwilling to part with him, and therefore has made overtures, which it is supposed that admirable leader will accept, and resume the direction of the Opera Band. If CRAMER and GALLINI should coalesce once more, GIARDINI will conduct the Concerts at the Pantheon.'

16 March 1790

In the eve^g Phillips & I having tickets went to Hanover Square to Miss Abrams benefit, wch in point of company was a very good one – for the rest I had much pleasure in hearing Salomon – & some in hearing Miss Abrams – a younger sister, only 12 years old, wth a very sweet voice sang & played a harp^s lesson, for her *age, extremely* well.[2]

On 18 March, she made a point of attending the first Pantheon performance since her arrival in town:

In the eve^g went to the Pantheon wth M^r & Mrs Lock & the 3 young men, & 2 sweet girls, & Miss Angerstein – we were shortly joined by Esther & our pretty niece, & we had a very exquisite Musical Feast – Bianchi the tenor singer, tho' wth a very bad cold, pleased me greatly – He has a very fine style of singing, & a fine theatrical voice, tho' now clouded & husky by his cold – Weichsell is a neat, rapid, yet cold player – I did not like his tone, & of feeling he seems to have none – Mr B. played charmingly & I was delighted to hear Fischer, who was very sweet, tho' alas, I perceive his powers decay – his breath is short, & his fingers are losing the spring of youth – but in a pastoral pathetic movement he is still all that can be wished.

The programming of songs during the 1790 Pantheon season was structured in a fairly consistent manner. For each concert in which they performed, Benda, Bianchi, Graziani, Dechasteau and Kreisel were allotted two songs. Pacchierotti alone sometimes performed three. Susan considered herself fortunate to be present on a night when her favourite sang an additional piece. In the published programme his songs were advertised as being by Sacchini, Giordani and Paisiello. She was notably unimpressed with Weichsell, a violinist whose performance she deemed cold and unfeeling. Fischer, the oboist, could still enthral, even though his powers were now diminishing with age.

The following night, Susan attended an important benefit, that of the violinist Giornovichi, who had recently arrived in London and was taking part in some concerts organized by Dussek. She gives a splendid account of the impact of this outstanding player. Having experienced the overwhelming power and musical presence of a true virtuoso, she could justify her pleasure in Salomon and Scheener, obviously lesser lights, only by categorizing them as chamber players. It is a distinction of some significance.

19 March 1790

It was Giornovichi's Benefit, & very much crowded – the applause he rec^d something like that wch was given to Gabrielli on her first appearance – his singers were Mrs Pieltain, Bianchi, & Storace – Dussec played a Lesson very finely, & a much more pleasing composition than that we afterwards heard together at Titchfield Street – I was very curious to hear him – I remember

[2]   New York Public Library, Berg Collection, Susanna E. B. Phillips, holograph diary for 1786–92.

nothing else that particularly pleased me – except Giornovichi's Concerto's – He played 2 – & really wonderfully – execution – spirit – power – delicacy – precision can go no further – in point of Fire & Fancy I think Salamon does not yield to him – & in touching expression, & a taste & judgment wch never err, Scheener is I think still unique on his instrument – Altogether however I sh^d not scruple to say that Giornovichi seems to me the greatest violinist I have ever heard – & tho' I will *privately* own to you (for it w^d be treason sh^d our dear father hear it) that I do not think *he c^d* give me the exquisite sensation of pleasure I have sometimes received from hearing Scheener – He certainly excells not only him but all others I have heard in all the mechanical parts of the art, & is besides I believe an Enthusiast & a genius – In *public*, & in playing a *Concerto* I believe I sh^d choose him before all others – At *Norbury*, & to accompany the Piano Forte undoubtedly my first wish w^d be for Scheener (Salamon was among the audience & a most warm applauder – & Scheener met me coming out, who spoke wth the highest praise of their great Rival's powers).

It is noteworthy that both Salomon and Scheener were present, doubtless to evaluate this new competitor. From a purely selfish point of view, the enthusiastic applause given to Giornovichi could be seen as worrying. Indeed, the comparison with Gabrielli's début suggests that his playing caused a sensation.[3] But whatever their private views about the potential impact on their own careers, in public they were under an obligation to demonstrate good breeding by displaying generosity of spirit, and to be fair their positive reactions could have represented genuine appreciation.

The following week, Susan went to her second concert at the Pantheon, accompanied by Giornovichi and the composers Mortellari and Gyrowitz:

25 March 1790

We went – & in listening to Pacchierotti forgot that we had gone regretfully – Mr B. did not play a Concerto – & Pacchierotti sang only two songs – the concert therefore was less rich than that of the preceding Thursday – but Fischer was again sweet – & Pacchierotti never *could* sing more exquisitely – in the second act particularly, when he sang a long scene of recitative & an air by Sarti, wch was a most *captivating* and *bewitching* performance – Oh that you had heard him! ...

Dear Pacchierotti afterwards came to speak to me & Mortellari sate by me nearly the whole eve^g – of the former I had very little, tho' the satisfaction of perceiving his wish was to give me more & some others who assailed him less of his time – Giornovichi sate opposite me wth his back to the orchestra during the 2^d act, & seems a warm admirer of Pacchierotti – Girowitz the composer & he had a little amusement concerning the various merits of this exquisite singer & of Marchesi – Girowitz at last said, 'Eh bien, il est vrai que Pacchierotti est plus tendre mais Marchesi a plus de noblesse – Vous vous meprenez [replied] Giornovichi wth great quickness – Marchesi a de la *fierté* – mais c'est Pacchierotti qui chante avec noblesse' – I liked his distinction very much – & it served quite to silence his antagonist.

---

3   Woodfield, *Opera and Drama*, 126–35.

The behaviour of Giornovichi in sitting with the Burney party and in praising their favourite Pacchierotti is consistent with an ambition to promote himself as a future leader. Whether he intended any insult to Weichsell by sitting with his back to the stage – bearing in mind that his own name had been mentioned in the *Public Advertiser* on 16 November as a possible leader of the current series – must be left an open question, although it did not escape the sharp eye of his companion.

On 28 March, Susan attended a private concert at Titchfield Street, at which Salomon was one of the performers:

I found my dearest Girl at our Esther's – & our beloved friends – the Corris & Salomon wth his young protégé, who, tho I admired him very much, took up the time barbarously – It is cruel to think what my poor Fanny lost this eve^g – Made^e Krumpholz exceeded all my expectations & ideas – I think greater *perfection* I never heard on any instrument – nor anything perhaps so heavenly as was the adagio wth wch her concerto began – the music was Dussec's – & the same in wch I had heard him at Giornovichi's benefit – but tho' he played it wth a very fine & impassioned expression, Made^e Krumpholtz rendered it a million of times more pathetic & more celestial the dying sounds – The effect of distance wch she is able to produce in her diminuendos, have an effect that I cannot describe – but wch seemed to lift me to another sphere – Her lesson was so universally wished to be repeated, that a murmured encore by degrees gathered strength – & she had the good nature to comply with it – I w^d give a great deal indeed that you c^d have heard this performance.

Esther after this was accomp^d by Salomon in a lesson of Haydn's, wch was not coldly heard, tho' it was a great trial to follow immediately this Musical Divinity – She played charmingly but was not so much at her ease as I think completely to do herself justice – nothing failed in the execution – but in expression & nuances, it is necessary to be free from flurry to do as well as we are able – There was rather a stirring trio after this by the 3 Corris – all singing as loud as they could – at the Little Theatre in the Haymarket I think it might possibly have had a good effect.

The Room now thinned quickly – but Salomon at my request accomp^d himself charmingly in a little composition of his own wch he remembered by heart – & even after this Mrs Eckards prevailed on Mrs Krumpholtz to recollect an air wth variations by Mr St George, & she played yet another, wch concluded the eve^g's exquisite entertainment.

Undoubtedly the saddest musical encounter of Susan's 1790 spring visit to London was with Giardini. At one stage in the autumn of 1789, the ageing violinist had been tipped as leader of the Pantheon orchestra but, as Susan reports, his once compelling abilities were virtually gone:

After dinner my Father carried Esther & I into his study, where they played over some beautiful new duets by Pleyell – & this over we were summoned to Giardini, who had bro^t wth him *Laurenti*, his scholar the Opera Singer – & 3 men – one of whom played the tenor – the other c^d play a violoncello, but was never employed & the third was his *Priest*, as Mr Scott who came soon after assured us, & sat in a corner of the room all the eve^g very soberly – never opening his lips. Giardini is grown very old – is still amusing in the Bobaldil way – he told a number of stories wch w^d not have disgraced that character – such palpable, tho' often comical falsehoods, I have seldom heard ventured upon – Laurenti is young, & reckoned pretty – I conceive her to be like an *Otahateian* beauty – her complexion is perfectly olive – & her eyes as black as a kyroc's, & without any white in them – She seems to me part coquettish, & silly – She sung 2 songs wch did not disarm censure – her voice has nothing I think to distinguish or recommend it, & there is very little meaning tho' great affectation of expression in her singing . . .

Giardini accomp^d Esther in two lessons wch she played admirably – but he accomp^d vilely – his powers are almost wholly gone – he mistook the notes, scratched, & in short played like a bad *dilettante* performer.

In his Quartettos composed for himself in this his decline, he was better – but had indeed very little left of those musical abilities for which he has been so famed – his tone is only sweet in slow passages – his execution is wretched – & his taste old fashioned, & now at times inelegant almost to vulgarity – wth regard to feeling & expression I always tho^t him very deficient – & always considered him as a very mechanical player.

I c^d not help feeling a little melancholy at first in observing such a fall, tho' Giardini is no great favourite of mine – Many in the room however professed that they tho^t him divine – so common is it to take merit upon trust, & so few there are who can form any judgement for themselves . . .

Giardini's decline had been noticed several years earlier by John Marsh. Hearing him in the opera *Medonte* on 19 November 1782, he formed the opinion that the violinist was 'much gone off as to his execution', though 'sweetness of tone, great expression, beautiful simplicity of style' were still apparent.[4] It is interesting that Susan Burney not only thought his playing incompetent. She clearly viewed it as stylistically dated.

In the space of a few weeks, Susan had heard most of London's leading violinists. Her aesthetic preference for players who could convey warmth of feeling and expression never wavered, nor her dislike of cold, 'mechanical' players, amongst whom she put Cramer, Giardini and Weichsell.

---

4 *The John Marsh Journals*, ed. Robins, 274.

8

Salomon and Gallini

The orchestral contest between the two series at Hanover Square and the Pantheon in 1790 was merely a preliminary skirmish. In the longer term, the future of the rival concert series would depend on the outcome of the developing struggle between O'Reilly and the newly formed partnership between Taylor and Gallini over the right to stage Italian opera. As this fiercely fought contest intensified in the spring of 1790, it became clear that the result would depend on the outcome of two questions: (1) who would be awarded the licence; (2) who could build or rent an auditorium of sufficient size and quality first. The extraordinary duplicity that shrouded negotiations over the licence has been documented,[1] yet without a building the licence had little real value. When plans for a new opera house at Leicester Square fell through, O'Reilly and his backers turned to the Pantheon and a deal was quickly agreed. Burney reported the current state of the negotiations in a letter to his son dated 21 July 1790:

The Pantheon business has occupied much of my time & thoughts lately. It is I believe sure of being made into an opera house by Wyatt the original architect for OReiley to whom we have granted a lease for 12 years. He is supported by the Ld. Chamberlain, who is determined to grant no one else a licence ... He is to give 3000 G[uinea]s a year – wch. after our part of the Taxes is deducted will be upwards of £50 per ann. for each share. Pacchierotti & Mara are to be principal singers – Bianchi Tenor etc ... There will be a bustle abt. the building begun to be erected on the old scite [i.e. the Haymarket], but I believe the undertakers will be obliged to give it up for want of money to go on, & for want of a Licence if it shd. be finished.[2]

On 17 September Burney took Susan to see the Pantheon, which she reported was 'transforming into a Theatre'. She thought it would be 'very fine', but wondered 'how it may prove in point of convenience, or for the effect of the music'. The contracts for the leading singers were hastily issued, Pacchierotti's being dated 16 August.[3]

From Salomon's point of view, the crucial event to emerge from this period of turmoil was Cramer's decision to join O'Reilly. This heralded the seismic shift in allegiances which was so greatly to his benefit and which set the scene for Haydn's visit. No documentation survives concerning Cramer's recruitment, but like all his colleagues he had no

[1]   Price, Milhous and Hume, *Italian Opera*, i.
[2]   Curtis Price, 'Italian Opera and Arson in Late Eighteenth-Century London', *Journal of the American Musicological Society*, 42 (1989), 55–107 (p. 57).
[3]   *Ibid.*, 103.

reason to assume that the Lord Chamberlain would issue a licence for the Haymarket. Cramer's decision to leave Gallini can probably be dated to the period around late June or early July, when the agreement with the shareholders of the Pantheon gave a semblance of reality to O'Reilly's plans. At this point Gallini acted decisively, aligning himself with an alternative partner to replicate his long-standing agreement with Cramer. He had no time to lose in view of the imminence of the summer recruiting trip, all the more urgent this year since Pacchierotti and Mara were on the verge of signing up with O'Reilly. Thus it was that Salomon gave himself a chance to achieve what he had so long desired and what had so long eluded him: if Gallini was successful, he stood to gain the prestigious opera leadership, and with it access to high-quality stars of Italian opera for his own subscription series. Of even greater significance – though this could not have been predicted at the time – he inherited Gallini's well-established plan to bring over Haydn to compose for both the opera house and an associated concert series. Salomon doubtless jumped at the chance, even though the outcome of Gallini's struggle was uncertain. It was a wise decision that was to transform his career prospects. As to why Gallini opted for Salomon, there are a number of likely reasons. The pragmatic explanation is that he was available when needed. In the midst of all his other difficulties, Gallini was working to a very tight schedule between the end of the opera season and the start of his recruitment trip in August. Another factor could have been Salomon's substantial experience of the London concert world. If Gallini were to get his licence, it was a fair assumption that the 1791 season would be dominated by the competition between rival opera houses and rival subscription series, and this factor perhaps told against some of his rivals. The brilliant Giornovichi had only just arrived; Weichsell was still young, and had perhaps not been entirely convincing in the 1790 Pantheon series. In its review of the opening concert, *The Times*, generally favourable to the Pantheon, hinted that though 'his execution and stile displayed infinite taste', his bowing, while displaying 'much neatness', was 'not equal in strength of tone to either Jarnewich or Salomon'.[4] Weichsell also suffered from a sight problem. John Marsh, reporting the Winchester Festival in October 1790, wrote: 'The band [was] led by young Weichsell, a very good player, but so exceedingly nearsighted that he was forced to place his face down close to the book all the time which much took off from the effect.'[5] Giardini certainly had the experience but was clearly no longer employable in such a position. Salomon had one further asset that was about to be cashed in: the good relationship he had established with Haydn in 1790.

[4] *The Times*, 29 January 1790.
[5] *The John Marsh Journals*, ed. Robins, 481.

9

The Recruitment of Haydn: Fact and Legend

It is not known when Salomon left England for his fateful recruiting trip of 1790, but evidence from the Anglo-Indian Fowke family shows that he was still in London at the end of June.[1] Griesinger stated that Gallini divided responsibility for recruiting a cast of singers with Salomon, visiting Italy himself and leaving his partner to take an itinerary through Germany.[2] The opera impresario can have had no particular reason to suppose that Haydn would finally be given permission to travel, and yet, in view of his unwavering interest in the composer over the years, it is likely enough that he would have instructed Salomon to make yet another approach if there seemed any chance of success. In the famous story, however, Salomon's recruitment of Haydn was a piece of pure serendipity, occasioned by the fact that he had only reached Cologne on his return journey when he heard news of the death of the composer's employer on 28 September. In the light of the dealings between the two men in early 1790, Salomon's famous words upon meeting the composer – 'I am Salomon from London' – take on a slightly different innuendo: 'I am he who earlier this year offered you 40 ducats for a cantata!' For all Gallini's long campaign and his money, the successful conclusion of the contract came down to the warmth of Salomon's previous contacts with Haydn, the charm of his personality and the dynamism of his approach. The contract itself has not survived, and it is now impossible to adjudicate between the numerous irreconcilable versions of its contents that were subsequently reported.[3]

In England the perception quickly gained currency that Salomon was the sole recruiter. His celebrated announcement 'To the Musical

---

[1] Wimbledon, 21 June 1790, Francis Fowke to Margaret Benn: 'I had for some days been engaged to dine at Clapham at Mrs Davenport's. Salomon was there and Mrs Hodges, wife of the little solemn painter. I don't know whether you ever heard her. She plays very well and preludes in a masterly style. She is a daughter of a music-seller and taught before her marriage.' British Library, Oriental and India Office Collections, European MS D546/26.

[2] Georg August Griesinger, *Biographische Notizen über Joseph Haydn* (Leipzig, 1810), 34. 'Fürst Nikolaus Esterhazy starb am 28sten Sept. 1790, zu der Zeit, wo Gallini nach Italien gereist war, um Sänger, und unter den berühmten Davide zu seinem Londner Professionale Concert in Hanover-Square zu werben. Salomon war ebenfalls in Cölln auf der Rückreise nach London begriffen, nachdem er mehrere deutsche Tonkünstler für Gallini engagiert hatte.'

[3] McVeigh, 'The Professional Concert', 96.

World'[4] must be regarded as one of the most important musical publicity coups of the eighteenth century. Gallini's name is not mentioned at all:

Mr. SALOMON having taken a Journey to Vienna purposely to engage the celebrated HAYDN, Chapel-Master to his present Highness Prince ESTERHAZY, to come to England, most respectfully acquaints the Nobility and Gentry, that he has actually signed an agreement with Mr. Haydn; in consequence, they are to set out together from Vienna in a few Days, and hope to be in London before the end of December when Mr. Salomon will have the honour of submitting to the Publick a Plan of a Subscription Concert, which he flatters himself will meet with its Approbation and Encouragement.

Vienna, Dec. 8, 1790

Salomon's associate, the music-seller John Bland, may also have played a role, and it was to his shop at No. 45 Holborn that Haydn was first taken.[5] One other individual who may have been associated with the recruitment of Haydn was John Baptist Mara, to whom Salomon sent his announcement.[6] On 29 December it was reported in the *Gazetteer* that Madame Mara was to take part in Salomon's series after a disagreement with the Professional Concert.[7] Having sung for several years in opposition to the Professional Concert, Mara finally performed for them during the 1789–90 opera season. It is not known whether by doing so she had accepted one of Gallini's dual contracts. The relationship with Cramer did not last long. Now in dispute again with the Professional Concert, Mara was apparently willing to reach an agreement with Salomon. This was perhaps not a very realistic ambition, as it would have left her (unless she were willing to renege on her opera contract with O'Reilly) with loyalties divided between two very polarized camps. It has often been claimed that the Professional Concert mounted an anti-Haydn campaign in the first few days after his arrival.[8] At least some of this innuendo, however, seems to bear the imprint of the Mara faction, disappointed at the failure of Salomon to hire her. On 5 February, the *Gazetteer* concluded a piece about Haydn, 'the nine days wonder', as follows: 'How Mr. Haydn and his associate *Salomon* came to overlook the talents of Madame Mara in the formation of their orchestra, can only be accounted for from the proverbial *avarice* of Germany.'[9]

As the longer-term significance of Haydn's two visits to London gradually became apparent, interest in who made the all-important recruitment began to grow. For English writers, Salomon was the undisputed 'hero'. Gallini was forgotten, the wider purpose of the

[4] Landon, *Haydn in England*, 30.
[5] Woodfield, 'John Bland', 234–5.
[6] Landon, *Haydn in England*, 30.
[7] McVeigh, 'The Professional Concert', 97.
[8] Landon, *Haydn in England*, 42.
[9] *Ibid.*, 44.

recruiting trip (to hire singers) was overlooked, and emphasis was increasingly placed on the idea that Salomon went 'purposely' to Vienna to recruit Haydn, as though it had been the original intention of his trip all along rather than a fortunate by-product. Fanny Burney published the words of her father who knew as much as anyone did about the long campaign to bring Haydn to England:

This year [1791] was auspiciously begun, in the musical world, by the arrival in London of the illustrious Joseph Haydn. 'Tis to Salomon that the lovers of music are indebted for what the lovers of music will call this blessing. Salomon went over himself to Vienna, upon hearing of the death of the Prince of Esterhazy, the great patron of Haydn, purposely to tempt that celebrated musical genius hither.[10]

English historiography thus diverged at an early stage from the version of events recorded by the 'authentic' German Haydn biographers, who acknowledged Gallini's part and emphasized the fortuitous nature of the event.

A legend was in the making. In keeping with the temper of the early nineteenth century, English writers began to depict Salomon increasingly as a 'great man'. With Mozart's stature finally recognized in England, the author of the 'Memoir' interprets the recruitment as part of a grand plan to bring both great composers to England:

It was in 1790, that Salomon formed his project and digested his plan; and in order to give every possible effect as well as eclât to his concerts, he determined to engage Haydn and Mozart, not only to write exclusively for them, but to conduct their compositions in person. For this purpose he went to Vienna, where after several interviews with both these great musicians, it was mutually agreed that Haydn should go to London the first season, and Mozart the next. They all dined together on the day fixed for the departure of the travellers: Mozart attended them to the door of their carriage, wishing them every success, and repeating, as they drove off, his promise to complete his part of the agreement the following year.[11]

The tradition of the double recruitment plan, which stems ultimately from the stories published by Dies and Griesinger 20 years earlier,[12] enhanced still further Salomon's image as the man who could recognize real talent. There were some absurd attempts to claim some credit by association. 'Mr. Papendiek', it was asserted, 'handed [Salomon] into the carriage, when he set off for Vienna to engage either Mozart or Haydn for the ensuing winter.'[13] The English interpretation of Salomon's role in the affair gained credence because it provided a more

[10] Fanny Burney [Madame d'Arblay], *Memoirs of Dr Burney*, 3 vols. (London, 1832), iii, 132.
[11] Anon., 'Memoir', 45.
[12] There are, however, obvious inconsistencies between these sources. See *Haydn Studies: Proceedings of the International Haydn Conference*, ed. Jens Peter Larsen, Howard Serwer and James Webster (New York and London, 1981), 69.
[13] Papendiek, *Court and Private Life*, ii, 210.

satisfying conclusion to the long campaign to bring Haydn to London – the ten years of offers, negotiations, quarrels and reported agreements quickly denied – than the alternative explanation, that it was virtually a fluke and that the main component of the deal was a failed Italian opera. For a fairer perspective, it is necessary to insist that Gallini (as the major financier of the deal) was fully involved in the recruitment. Certainly, Haydn arrived in London expecting to start work immediately on an opera.

It has been argued during the course of this study that the initial suggestion that Haydn should be recruited to work jointly for the opera house and a subscription series came from Burney, and that his desire to revitalize the Italian cantata in England played some part in stimulating Salomon's contact with the composer in 1790. In the light of these findings, their first meeting takes on added significance. Busby noted:

Haydn had determined, that the first visit he paid in England, should be to an English musical professor; and accordingly selected Dr Burney, on whom, accompanied by Salomon, he, the next day after his arrival, called upon, at Chelsea Hospital. The Doctor, as sensible of the high compliment paid him as of the exalted merits of his visitor, received him with all the pleasure and all the attention natural to so flattering a circumstance; and a warm and mutual friendship was the result.[14]

The portrayal of this meeting as a kind of random whim on Haydn's part is unconvincing given the extent of Burney's involvement. The wily composer surely knew that behind the scenes his host was one of the most influential men in the London musical world.

If it was important to English writers to depict Salomon in a heroic light, it was equally necessary to demonstrate that London, rapidly assuming its position as imperial capital, was appropriately supportive of his efforts. The author of the 'Memoir' makes a rather pointed comparison with Paris. Although 'a city which has always been noted for its courtesy to artists of talent', Paris in Salomon's case was supposed to have been 'louder in applause than liberal in reward'. Only when he came to 'the wealthy metropolis of the British Empire' did he find the 'object of his search' (i.e. money), in which he was aided by an 'enterprising spirit' and regulated by 'great discretion'. The theme of Salomon as the risk-taking entrepreneur was taken up in the derivative entry in Sainsbury's *Dictionary*: 'This country is indebted to the spirit and enterprise of Salomon for having brought into it, at a great pecuniary risk, the most original, brilliant, and fertile genius that has appeared in our days, the immortal Haydn!'[15] While Salomon perhaps

14 Busby, *Concert Room and Orchestra*, ii, 269.
15 *A Dictionary of Musicians from the Earliest Times*, ed. John Sainsbury, 2 vols. (London, 1825; repr. 1966), ii, 411. On the patriotic aims of this dictionary, see Leanne Langley, 'Sainsbury's *Dictionary*, the Royal Academy of Music, and the Rhetoric of Patriotism', *Music and British Culture, 1785–1914: Essays in Honour of Cyril Ehrlich* (Oxford, 2000), 65–97.

did lose out financially in his first Hanover Square series with Haydn, in the long term the credit that accrued to his reputation far outweighed any such short-term loss.[16] Although clearly wishing to depict London as having been appropriately supportive of a fine artist – and there is perhaps here an unspoken comment on Vienna's tragic failure – the author of the 'Memoir' clearly felt that he had to account for the fact that Salomon had not amassed the considerable riches that he might have been expected to make. An element of anti-Semitism is recalled:

It was the fashion of the day, to accuse Salomon of being excessively mercenary; he was called a *Jew*. But the fact is, that, being liberal by nature, many attempts were made to take undue advantage of his good disposition, and these were too frequently successful.

Thus, rather conveniently, Salomon's universally acknowledged generosity was the explanation for his modest circumstances:

his purse was so readily opened when his compassion was excited, that if his very faithful and vigilant servant, who lived with him twenty-eight years, had not been more cautious than his master, the latter would, in all probability, long before his death, have offered his independence at the shrine of charity.[17]

A career as a top professional violinist in London might take time to establish and might last for many years, but when the decline set in it was very difficult to reverse. The evidence presented in this study suggests that prior to his triumph in 1791 Salomon's position was under real threat. After several years of relative decline, the low point came in 1789 with a series of reverses: the disappointing benefit; the reduced concert series in Dublin; and the failure to get the Pantheon leadership. Salomon owed the extraordinary recovery in his position to the coincidence of two unrelated but highly significant events – the destruction of the King's Theatre and the death of Nikolaus Esterházy. Little more than a year after his weekend in Surrey, he was knocking at another door, with the celebrated words: 'Ich bin Salomon aus London, und komme, Sie abzuholen.'

---

[16]   McVeigh, 'The Professional Concert', 96–7.
[17]   Anon, 'Memoir', 45, 47.

Bibliography

SUSAN BURNEY MSS

New York Public Library, Berg Collection, Susanna E. B. Phillips, holograph
    diary for 1786–92
British Library, Egerton MS 3692, journal-letters 1787–95
Armagh Public Library, copies of 27 journal-letters from Susan to Fanny Burney,
    1787–8, catalogued as Mrs Molesworth Phillips, Letters, i; copies of 52
    journal-letters from Susan to Fanny Burney, 1795–9, catalogued as Mrs
    Molesworth Phillips, Letters, ii

WEBSITE

http://www.nottingham.ac.uk/hrc/projects/burney

BOOKS AND ARTICLES

Anon., 'Memoir of Johann Peter Salomon', *Harmonicon*, 8 (1830), 45–7
Barrett, Charlotte (ed.), *Diary and Letters of Madame D'Arblay (1778–1840)*,
    introduction and notes by Austin Dobson, 6 vols. (London, 1904–5)
Boydell, Brian, *Rotunda Music in Eighteenth-Century Dublin* (Dublin, 1992)
Burney, Charles, *A General History of Music from the Earliest Ages to the Present
    Period*, ed. Frank Mercer, 2 vols. (London, 1935; repr. 1957)
Burney, Fanny [Madame d'Arblay], *Memoirs of Dr Burney*, 3 vols. (London,
    1832)
Burney, Fanny, *The Early Journals and Letters*, ed. Lars E. Troide, ii (Oxford, 1990)
Busby, Thomas, *Concert Room and Orchestra: Anecdotes of Music and Musicians,
    Ancient and Modern*, 3 vols. (London, 1825)
Gardiner, William, *Music and Friends*, 2 vols. (London, 1838)
Gibson, Elizabeth, 'Earl Cowper in Florence and his Correspondence with the
    Italian Opera in London', *Music and Letters*, 67 (1987), 235–52
Griesinger, Georg August, *Biographische Notizen über Joseph Haydn* (Leipzig,
    1810)
Haydn, Joseph, *Gesammelte Briefe und Aufzeichnungen*, ed. H. C. Robbins Landon
    and Dénes Bartha (Kassel, 1965)
Hemlow, Joyce, *The History of Fanny Burney* (Oxford, 1958)
Highfill, Philip H., Jr, Kalman A Burnim and Edward A. Langhans, *A
    Biographical Dictionary of Actors, Actresses, Musicians, Dancers, Managers
    and Other Stage Personnel in London 1660–1800*, 16 vols. (Carbondale,
    1973–93)
Hill, Mary Constance (ed.), *The House in St Martin's Street: Being Chronicles of the
    Burney Family* (London and New York, 1907)
Hogan, Ita, *Anglo-Irish Music* (Cork, 1966)
Landon, H. C. Robbins, *Haydn in England 1791–1795* (London, 1976)
——, *Haydn at Esterháza 1766–1790* (London, 1978)
——, 'Four New Haydn Letters', *Haydn Yearbook*, 13 (1982), 213–19
——, 'More Haydn Letters in Autograph', *Haydn Yearbook*, 14 (1983), 200–5

——, 'Zu den Haydn-Autographen der Sammlung Paul Sacher', *Komponisten des 20. Jahrhunderts in der Paul Sacher Stiftung* (Basle, 1986), 31–6

——, 'Haydn und die Familie Bertie', *Österreichische Musik Zeitschrift*, 43 (1988), 21–4

Langley, Leanne, 'Sainsbury's *Dictionary*, the Royal Academy of Music, and the Rhetoric of Patriotism', *Music and British Culture, 1785–1914: Essays in Honour of Cyril Ehrlich* (Oxford, 2000), 65–97

Larsen, Jens Peter, Howard Serwer and James Webster (eds.), *Haydn Studies: Proceedings of the International Haydn Conference* (New York and London, 1981)

McVeigh, Simon, *The Violinist in London's Concert Life* (New York, 1989)

——, *Concert Life in London from Mozart to Haydn* (Cambridge, 1993)

——, 'The Professional Concert and Rival Subscription Series in London, 1783–1793', *Research Chronicle of the Royal Musical Association*, 22 (1989), 1–136

Milhous, Judith, and Robert D. Hume, 'Opera Salaries in Eighteenth-Century London', *Journal of the American Musicological Society*, 46 (1993), 26–83

——, Gabriella Dideriksen and Robert D. Hume, *Italian Opera in Late Eighteenth-Century London*, ii: *The Pantheon Opera and its Aftermath, 1790–1795* (Oxford, 2001)

Oldman, Cecil B., 'Haydn's Quarrel with the "Professionals" in 1788', *Musik und Verlag: Karl Vötterle zum 65. Geburtstag am 12. April 1968*, ed. Richard Baum and Wolfgang Rehm (Kassel, 1968), 459–65

Papendiek, Charlotte, *Court and Private Life in the Time of Queen Charlotte: Being the Journals of Mrs Papendiek, Assistant Keeper of the Wardrobe and Reader to her Majesty, Edited by her Grand-Daughter, Mrs Vernon Delves Broughton*, 2 vols. (London, 1887)

Parke, William T., *Musical Memoirs*, 2 vols. (London, 1830)

Price, Curtis, 'Italian Opera and Arson in Late Eighteenth-Century London', *Journal of the American Musicological Society*, 42 (1989), 55–107

——, Judith Milhous and Robert D. Hume, *Italian Opera in Late Eighteenth-Century London*, i: *The King's Theatre, Haymarket, 1778–1791* (Oxford, 1995)

Reid, Douglas J., and Brian Pritchard, 'Some Festival Programmes of the Eighteenth and Nineteenth Centuries: 1. Salisbury and Winchester; 2. Cambridge and Oxford; 3. Liverpool and Manchester', *Research Chronicle of the Royal Musical Association*, 5 (1965), 51–79; 6 (1966), 3–22; 7 (1967), 1–27

Ribeiro, Alvaro (ed.), *The Letters of Charles Burney*, i: *1751–1784* (Oxford, 1991)

Robins, Brian (ed.), *The John Marsh Journals: The Life and Times of a Gentleman Composer (1752–1828)* (Stuyvesant, NY, 1998)

Rohr, Deborah A., 'A Profession of Artisans: The Careers and Social Status of British Musicians 1750–1850' (Ph.D. dissertation, University of Pennsylvania, 1983)

Roscoe, Christopher, 'Haydn and London in the 1780s', *Music and Letters*, 49 (1968), 203–12

Sadie, Stanley, and John Tyrrell (eds.), *The New Grove Dictionary of Music and Musicians*, 29 vols. (2nd, rev. edn., London, 2001)

Sainsbury, John (ed.), *A Dictionary of Musicians from the Earliest Times*, 2 vols. (London, 1825; repr. 1966)

Sermoneta, The Duchess of, *The Locks of Norbury* (London, 1940)

Stowell, Robin, 'Johann Peter Salomon – Director or Co-ordinator?', *Newsletter of the Haydn Society of Great Britain*, 8 (1988), 9

Woodfield, Ian, 'New Light on the Mozarts' London Visit: A Private Concert with Manzuoli', *Music and Letters*, 65 (1995), 187–208

——, 'John Bland: London Retailer of the Music of Haydn and Mozart', *Music and Letters*, 81 (2000), 210–44

——, *Music of the Raj: A Social and Economic History of Music in Late Eighteenth-Century Anglo-Indian Society* (Oxford, 2000)

——, *Opera and Drama in Eighteenth-Century London: The King's Theatre, Garrick and the Business of Performance* (Cambridge, 2001)

Index